THE APARTMENT BOOK
APARTMENTS. EXKLUSIVE EINRICHTUNGSIDEEN
HET APPARTEMENTENBOEK
EL GRAN LIBRO DE LOS APARTAMENTOS

THE APARTMENT BOOK
APARTMENTS. EXKLUSIVE EINRICHTUNGSIDEEN
HET APPARTEMENTENBOEK
EL GRAN LIBRO DE LOS APARTAMENTOS

Yolanda Martínez

FKG

FKG

Editorial project:
2011 © LOFT Publications
Via Laietana, 32, 4º, Of. 92
08003 Barcelona, Spain
Tel.: +34 932 688 088
Fax: +34 932 687 073
loft@loftpublications.com
www.loftpublications.com

Created and distributed in cooperation
with Frechmann Kolón GmbH
www.frechmann.com

Editorial coordinator:
Simone K. Schleifer

Assistant to editorial coordination:
Aitana Lleonart Triquell

Editor:
Yolanda Martínez

Art director:
Mireia Casanovas Soley

Design and layout coordination:
Claudia Martínez Alonso

Cover layout:
María Eugenia Castell Carballo

Layout:
Guillermo Pfaff Puigmartí

Photography:
Jordi Miralles

Translations:
Cillero & de Motta
Mengès (FR)

ISBN 978-84-9936-820-7 (GB)
ISBN 978-84-9936-818-4 (D)
ISBN 978-84-9936-821-4 (NL)
ISBN 978-84-9936-819-1 (E)

Printed in China

Traditionally, living in an apartment was thought of as a provisional arrangement; however it is becoming a very valid formula due to the increase in price of urban land. It is a relatively new concept and is already largely implemented in the modern world. Historically, rich people typically lived in brick houses or mansions, and the poor in shacks. It was not until the nineteenth century that residential neighborhoods with blocks of eclectic apartments sprung up for crowded cities and opted for high-rise construction, to the detriment of the traditional one storey houses.

An apartment is defined by the fact that it forms part of a building where there are other similar residential units, and consists of one or more bedrooms, kitchen and washroom. In general there is not a lot of space. Although it is common, a lack of space is not always the case- the content of this book confirms the existence of apartments ranging from five hundred square feet to over two thousand, depending on family needs, which sometimes are for a single person or a family with children – however this does mean that the interior designer or decorator has to think hard to come up with ideas that optimize the use of available space. Owning a house less than one thousand square feet does not mean you have to sacrifice style, decoratively speaking.

Another defining feature, but it is not always gospel either, is that they are used temporarily or as a vacation home. Typically, these homes located in tourist resorts, by the beach or in the mountains, used as a second home mean that the spaces have limited stylistic aspirations. Due to the fact they are located away from large cities, they often offer wonderful exterior views and the furniture in the house is organized around large windows or balconies that flood the interior with natural light.

What is common to all apartments is a clear strategy to create a lifestyle that suits the occupants of the house, reflecting the personality and tastes of those who live there through the furniture, accessories, materials, colors, fabrics, etc. In some cases the ambience is minimalist and simple, in others there is a more sophisticated aesthetic, but in most cases, at a glance we can tell a lot about the occupants without even knowing them. These interiors present a fascinating fusion of styles and objects, a synthesis of art and furniture or the past, fond memories and functional objects that combined harmoniously create a warm and comfortable home, full of significance. Thus, all inhabited space tells its story and the story of the people who live there, and who have pervaded their character in each of the corners.

What makes an apartment special is the balance between the pieces of furniture and the space, as well as their relationship with other architectural elements, which together form a balanced and comfortable place to live. In the majority of the cases, we are dealing with small interiors, thus the selection of small-scale furniture and light colors with minimal contrast is preferred.

The apartments featured in this book offer a wide variety of solutions to suit a vast variety of types: from small studios to large, industrial style spacious lofts, including duplexes, bungalows, showing the latest trends in national and international contemporary design. Many ideas and styles are a source of inspiration for anyone interested in interior design. In short, a journey through new decorating trends with classic, traditional, new and innovative styles that will appeal to all lovers of interior décor.

Traditionell verband man das Leben in einer Wohnung mit dem Gedanken an ein Provisorium, denn diese Art von Zuhause ist eine Formel, die aus der Teuerung der Grundstückspreise hervorgegangen ist. Wohnungen sind zwar ein fester Bestandteil unserer heutigen Welt, doch ihre Geschichte ist noch relativ jung. Früher lebten die wohlhabenderen Menschen in Häusern aus Ziegeln, während die ärmeren Schichten in Hütten wohnten. Erst im 19. Jahrhundert entstanden in den dicht besiedelten Städten die ersten Viertel mit zahlreichen Wohnblocks und man begann mit dem Bau von Häusern mit mehreren Etagen, im Gegensatz zu den früheren Häusern mit nur einem Geschoss.

Eine Wohnung ist ein Teil eines Gebäudes, in welchem mehrere oder viele ähnliche Wohneinheiten untergebracht sind, und besteht für gewöhnlich aus einem oder mehreren Aufenthalts- und Schlafräumen mit begrenzter Fläche, einer Küche und einem Bad. Beim Blättern in diesem Band werden Sie neben Apartments von 50 m², jedoch durchaus auch 200 m² große Wohnungen entdecken, da die Größe eines Zuhauses stets von den individuellen Bedürfnissen der jeweiligen Bewohner abhängt – teils handelt es sich um Einzelpersonen, in anderen Fällen um Familien mit Kindern. Stets jedoch stellen Wohnungsgröße und Bewohnerzahl den Innenarchitekten vor eine Herausforderung: er muss sich den Kopf zerbrechen und Ideen kreieren, um die Raumnutzung zu optimieren. Schließlich bedeutet eine Wohnung mit weniger als 100 m² Wohnfläche keineswegs, dass man auf eine gut gestylte Ausstattung verzichten muss.

Ein weiteres Merkmal von Wohnungen, das sehr häufig, jedoch nicht in allen Fälle zutrifft, ist ihre Nutzung als Zweit- bzw. Ferienwohnsitz, insbesondere bei Apartments in Urlaubsregionen, am Strand oder in den Bergen. Die Nutzung einer Immobilie als Zweitwohnung bringt es mit sich, dass meist weniger hohe Ansprüche an Einrichtung und Dekoration gestellt werden. Da diese Wohneinheiten außerhalb der großen Städte liegen, wird eine gute Aussicht ins Freie bevorzugt, und die Möbel werden um die großen Fenster oder Balkone gruppiert, welche viel Tageslicht in die Räume einfallen lassen.

In Wohnungen aller Art wird darauf abgezielt, ein Ambiente zu kreieren, das auf die Bewohner abgestimmt ist und deren Persönlichkeit und Geschmack widerspiegelt – sei es durch die verwendeten Möbel, Accessoires, Materialien, Farben oder Stoffe. Bisweilen wird eine minimalistische Ausstattung mit klaren Linien und schlichter Ästhetik vorgezogen, während in anderen Fällen eine edlere Gestaltung mit mehr Zierelementen vorherrscht. Eines ist jedoch stets sicher: Jede Wohnung gibt bereits auf den ersten Blick vieles über ihre Bewohner preis.

Die vorgestellten Interieurs zeigen eine faszinierende Fusion von Stilrichtungen und Einrichtungsgegenständen, eine Mischung aus avantgardistischen und antiken Möbeln, lieb gewonnenen Erinnerungsstücken und funktionellen Elementen, die – gekonnt miteinander kombiniert – ein wohnliches und komfortables Heim schaffen. Jede Wohnung erzählt ihre eigene Geschichte und die ihrer Bewohner, welche jeden einzelnen Winkel mit ihrer Persönlichkeit geprägt haben.

Was eine Wohnung zu einem besonderen Zuhause macht, ist ein harmonisches Gleichgewicht von Möbeln und Raum sowie ihre Beziehung zu den restlichen architektonischen Elementen. All dies zusammengenommen bildet ein komfortables Ganzes. Da es sich in den meisten Fällen um kleine Wohnflächen handelt, werden kleine, helle Möbelstücke mit wenig Farbkontrasten bevorzugt.

Die in diesem Band gezeigten Wohnungen bieten eine große Anzahl von Lösungen für die unterschiedlichsten Wohnungstypen. Vom kleinen Studio über Maisonettewohnungen und Bungalows bis hin zu großräumigen, industriell anmutenden Lofts... wir zeigen alle Trends des zeitgenössischen Designs auf nationaler und internationaler Ebene. Die zahlreichen Ideen und Stile dienen allen, die sich für das Thema Inneneinrichtung interessieren, als Quelle der Inspiration. Entdecken Sie die neuesten Trends und innovative Lösungen für klassische, traditionelle und moderne Wohnstile!

Traditionnellement, vivre dans un appartement était naguère considéré comme une disposition provisoire. Cependant, cela devient une formule très valable, compte tenu de la hausse du prix des terrains dans les villes. Le concept est relativement nouveau et il est déjà largement mis en œuvre dans le monde moderne. Historiquement, les riches vivaient dans des maisons de pierre ou de brique, ou bien dans des hôtels particuliers ; les pauvres, dans des cabanes. Il a fallu attendre le XIXe siècle pour voir naître des banlieues résidentielles, avec des immeubles d'appartements définissant des cités nouvelles, optant alors pour des constructions en hauteur au détriment des maisons traditionnelles à un étage.

Un appartement est défini par le fait qu'il fait partie d'un bâtiment où existent d'autres unités d'habitation du même type ; il est généralement constitué d'une ou plusieurs chambres, d'une cuisine et d'une salle de bains. En général, l'espace est assez limité, mais cette caractéristique n'est pas toujours valable : le contenu de cet ouvrage confirme l'existence d'appartements allant de 50 m^2 à plus de 200 m^2, en fonction des ressources et des besoins de la famille. Il peut s'agir par ailleurs d'une personne seule ou d'une famille avec enfants. Toutefois, cela ne signifie pas que le styliste ou décorateur d'intérieur doive se torturer les méninges pour produire des idées capables d'optimiser l'utilisation de l'espace disponible. Ainsi, la possession d'un habitat de moins de 100 m^2 n'implique pas que l'on doive renoncer à tout style dans la décoration intérieure.

Une autre caractéristique – mais qui n'est pas non plus universelle – est que les appartements sont souvent utilisés temporairement ou comme résidence de vacances. Typiquement, ces logements situés dans les localités touristiques – à la mer comme à la montagne – et utilisés comme résidences secondaires, impliquent que lesdits espaces ont nécessairement des ambitions stylistiques limitées. Étant donné que ces résidences sont situées loin des grandes villes, elles offrent souvent de merveilleuses vues extérieures et l'aménagement de ces appartements est organisé autour de grandes fenêtres et de balcons qui laissent pénétrer des flots de lumière à l'intérieur.

Ce qui est commun à tous les appartements est une stratégie définie pour créer un style de vie qui convienne aux occupants de la maison, reflétant la personnalité et les goûts de ceux qui vivent ici par le mobilier, les accessoires, les couleurs, les tissus, etc. Dans certains cas, l'ambiance est minimaliste et simple ; dans d'autres existe une esthétique plus sophistiquée, mais dans la plupart des cas, on peut dire au premier coup d'œil beaucoup de choses sur les occupants sans même les connaître. Ces intérieurs offrent un mélange fascinant de styles et d'objets, une synthèse de l'art et des mobiliers du passé, intégrant les souvenirs et des objets fonctionnels, harmonieusement combinés pour obtenir un foyer chaud et confortable, rempli de signification. Ainsi, tout espace habité raconte son histoire et celle des gens qui y vivent et qui ont empreint de leur caractère chaque coin de cet espace.

Ce qui fait la spécificité d'un appartement est l'équilibre entre l'espace et les éléments d'ameublement, aussi bien que leur relation avec d'autres éléments architecturaux ; la combinaison de tous ces éléments forme un lieu de vie équilibré et confortable. Dans la majorité des cas, nous avons affaire à de petits intérieurs, ce qui implique de privilégier des mobiliers de petite taille et des couleurs claires à contraste minimal.

Les appartements ici présentés offrent une grande diversité de solutions pour convenir à une grande variété de types : des petits studios aux vastes lofts de style industriel, y compris les duplex et les bungalows, traduisant les dernières tendances du stylisme contemporain international. Nombre d'idées et de styles pourront être des sources d'inspiration pour tous ceux qui s'intéressent au stylisme d'intérieur. En bref, il vous est proposé ici un voyage à travers les nouvelles tendances de la décoration intérieure, avec des solutions classiques, traditionnelles, nouvelles ou novatrices qui en séduiront tous les amateurs.

Vanouds werd het wonen in een appartement gezien als iets tijdelijks. De appartementen zoals wij die kennen zijn het resultaat van het duurder worden van de stedelijke bouwgrond. Deze ontwikkeling is relatief recent en is grotendeels geïmplanteerd in de moderne wereld. Door de geschiedenis heen woonden de rijken gewoonlijk in stenen huizen en landhuizen en de armen in hutten. Pas in de 19de eeuw kwamen de woonwijken met eclectische flatgebouwen in compacte steden in opkomst en werd er gekozen voor hoogbouw, ten koste van de traditionele huizen met een woonlaag.

Een appartement kan worden omschreven als een wooneenheid die deel uitmaakt van een gebouw waarin zich andere, gelijkwaardige eenheden bevinden; het bestaat uit een of meerdere kamers, een keuken en badkamer en heeft normaal gesproken geringe afmetingen. Hoewel dat wel gebruikelijk is, heeft het niet per definitie een beperkt oppervlak. Bladerend door dit boek vindt u appartementen van vijftig tot tweehonderd vierkante meter, hetgeen afhankelijk is van de behoeften van de bewoners, bijvoorbeeld een eenpersoons huishouden of een gezin met kinderen. Binnenhuisarchitecten en decorateurs moeten echter hun hersens wel meer pijnigen om ideeën op te doen om de beschikbare ruimte optimaal te benutten. Wonen in een huis van minder dan honderd vierkante meter betekent niet dat men hoeft af te zien van stijl, voor wat de inrichting betreft.

Een ander kenmerk is het gebruik van het appartement in de vakantie of voor een korte periode, hoewel dat niet altijd het geval is. Het gaat dan vaak om woningen die in toeristische enclaves, aan het strand of in de bergen liggen en waarin op stilistisch vlak weinig ambitie wordt nagestreefd omdat ze als tweede huis gebruikt worden. Doordat ze zich uit de buurt van de grote steden bevinden is het uitzicht belangrijk en worden de meubels opgesteld voor grote ramen of balkons waardoor het daglicht naar binnen schijnt.

Wat alle woningen wel gemeen hebben is een vastomlijnde strategie waarmee een levensstijl wordt gecreëerd die past bij de bewoners van het huis. Hun persoonlijkheid en smaak komen terug in het meubilair, de accessoires, materialen, kleuren, stoffering, etc. In enkele gevallen wordt gekozen voor een minimalistische entourage en een sobere uitstraling, terwijl in andere uiting wordt gegeven aan een verfijnde esthetiek. In beide gevallen kan men echter in een oogopslag veel over de inwoners vertellen, zonder hen echt te kennen. Deze interieurs geven blijk van een fascinerende mengeling van stijlen en voorwerpen, een kruising tussen ultramoderne of juist klassieke meubels, dierbare herinneringen en functionele voorwerpen die harmonieus met elkaar combineren en een warme en comfortabele woning, vol nuances vormen. Zo vertelt iedere ruimte zijn eigen geschiedenis en die van degenen die er wonen, wier karakter uit ieder hoekje spreekt.

Wat een appartement zo speciaal maakt is het evenwicht tussen het meubilair en de ruimte, alsmede het verband met de overige architectonische elementen, die samen een evenwichtig en comfortabel geheel vormen. Omdat het meestal om interieurs met een beperkt oppervlak gaat, gaat de voorkeur uit naar kleine meubels met heldere kleuren en een minimaal contrast.

De appartementen die wij hier laten zien bieden een uitgebreide reeks oplossingen die overeen komen met een enorme typologische verscheidenheid: vanaf kleine studio's tot ruime en riante lofts met industriële esthetiek, met daar tussenin duplexwoningen en bungalows, die de laatste trends in eigentijds design uit binnen- en buitenland laten zien. Er worden talrijke ideeën en stijlen aan de hand gedaan die een bron van inspiratie zullen vormen voor iedereen die belangstelling heeft voor binnenhuisarchitectuur. Het is, kortom, een overzicht van de nieuwe interieurtrends met klassieke, traditionele en moderne, doch altijd vernieuwende stijlen, die liefhebbers van woninginrichting niet onverschillig zal laten.

Tradizionalmente, vivere in un appartamento veniva associato alla provvisorietà, come conseguenza di una formula nata dal rincaro del suolo urbano. Tale svolgimento è relativamente recente ed è ormai generalmente impiantato nel mondo contemporaneo. Storicamente, i ricchi vivevano di solito in case fatte di mattoni o in mansioni, mentre i poveri in capanne. È nel secolo XIX quando sorgono i quartieri residenziali con caseggiati eclettici nelle città con alta densità di popolazione e si opta per edifici alti, sacrificando le tradizionali case su un unico piano.

Un appartamento, per definizione, forma parte di un edificio nel quale coesistono altre unità residenziali simili e consta di una o varie stanze, cucina e bagno, generalmente di ridotte dimensioni. La scarsezza di metri quadrati non è, per quanto sia abituale, un qualcosa di definitore – sfogliando le pagine di questo libro potrete osservare appartamenti che vanno dai cinquanta fino a duecento metri quadrati, a seconda delle necessità, alcuni per una sola persona altri per famiglie con figli –, ma spinge l'arredatore o il decoratore a cercare idee che ottimizzino l'uso dello spazio disponibile. Avere una casa con meno di cento metri quadrati non significa dover rinunciare allo stile nella decorazione.

Un'altra caratteristica principale, anche se non sempre è così, è il loro uso turistico o temporaneo. Normalmente, si tratta di case situate in zone turistiche, al mare o in montagna, il cui impiego come seconda casa determina uno spazio con limitate aspirazioni stilistiche. Lontano dalle grandi città, privilegiano le viste panoramiche e l'arredamento della casa si articola intorno a grandi finestre o balconi che inondano l'ambiente interno di luce naturale.

Ciò che le accomuna è una strategia definita per creare uno stile di vita che si adatti a quello degli abitanti della casa, che rifletti la personalità e i gusti di colui che lì vive attraverso l'arredamento, gli accessori, i materiali, i colori, i tessuti, ecc. In alcuni casi si opta per ambienti minimalisti e d'apparenza sobria, in altri troviamo estetiche sofisticate ma, sia in un caso che nell'altro, con una semplice occhiata si potrebbero dedurre molte cose sui suoi abitanti senza conoscerli. Questi ambienti interni espongono un affascinante fusione di stili e di oggetti, incrocio di mobili di avanguardia o del passato, dolci ricordi e oggetti funzionali che, combinati armoniosamente, formano una casa accogliente e comoda, piena de sfumature. E così, l'intera area abitata racconta la sua storia e quella delle persone che la vivono, e che hanno impregnato ogni angolo del loro carattere.

Ciò che rende speciale un appartamento è l'equilibrio tra i mobili e lo spazio, così come il raffronto con il resto degli elementi architettonici, che nell'insieme formano uno spazio equilibrato e confortevole da vivere. Trattandosi, soprattutto, di piccoli ambienti, si favorisce la scelta di mobili di piccole dimensioni e colori chiari, con il minimo contrasto.

Gli appartamenti qui presentati offrono un'ampia varietà di soluzioni adeguate ad una enorme ricchezza tipologica: da piccoli studi a vasti e spaziosi loft, d'estetica industriale, passando per duplex, bungalow, che mostrano le ultime tendenze del design contemporaneo nazionale e internazionale. Numerose idee e stili che costituiscono una fonte d'ispirazione per qualsiasi persona interessata all'arredamento. In definitiva, un percorso attraverso le nuove tendenze della decorazione con stili classici, tradizionali, nuovi, ma sempre innovatori e che non lasceranno indifferenti gli amanti della decorazione.

Tradicionalmente, vivir en un apartamento se ha considerado una solución provisional. Y es que, tal como los conocemos, los apartamentos son una fórmula nacida del encarecimiento del suelo urbano. Su historia es relativamente reciente y ya están mayoritariamente implantados en el mundo contemporáneo. Históricamente, los ricos solían vivir en casas de ladrillo o mansiones y los pobres, en cabañas o chabolas. No es hasta el siglo XIX que surgen los barrios residenciales con bloques de pisos eclécticos para las ciudades densamente pobladas y se opta por la construcción en altura, en detrimento de las casas tradicionales de una planta.

Lo que caracteriza a un apartamento es que forma parte de un edificio en el que hay otras unidades residenciales similares y consta de una o varias habitaciones, cocina y cuarto de baño, generalmente de reducidas dimensiones. Esta escasez de metros cuadrados no es, por habitual que sea, algo tan definitorio –las páginas de este libro incluyen desde apartamentos de cincuenta metros cuadrados hasta otros de doscientos, dependiendo de las necesidades de los inquilinos, según se trate de personas que viven solas o familias con hijos–, pero sí obligan al interiorista o decorador a exprimirse más la cabeza tratando de conseguir ideas que optimicen el espacio disponible. Tener una casa de menos de cien metros cuadrados no significa tener que renunciar al estilo en la decoración.

Otro rasgo definitorio, aunque tampoco se cumple siempre, es su uso vacacional o temporal. Normalmente, son viviendas situadas en enclaves turísticos, en la playa o en la montaña, cuya función como segunda residencia hace que se trate de espacios con limitadas aspiraciones estilísticas. Al estar apartados de las grandes urbes, dan prioridad a las vistas al exterior y los muebles de la casa se articulan alrededor de grandes ventanas o balcones que inundan el interior de luz natural.

Lo que sí es común en todos ellos es una estrategia definida para crear un estilo de vida que se adapte a los ocupantes de la casa, que refleje la personalidad y los gustos de quien vive ahí a través del mobiliario, los accesorios, los materiales, los colores, los tejidos, etc. En algunos casos se opta por ambientes minimalistas y de apariencia sobria, mientras que otras veces nos encontramos con estéticas sofisticadas; pero tanto en unos como en otros, con un simple vistazo al apartamento se podrían decir muchas cosas de sus ocupantes sin apenas conocerlos. Estos interiores exponen una fascinante fusión de estilos y objetos, mezcla de muebles de vanguardia o del pasado, recuerdos entrañables y objetos funcionales que, combinados armónicamente, integran una casa cálida y cómoda, llena de matices. De este modo, todo espacio habitado relata su historia y la de la gente que allí vive y que ha impregnado su carácter en cada uno de los rincones.

Lo que hace de un apartamento algo especial es el equilibrio entre las piezas de mobiliario y el espacio, así como su relación con el resto de elementos arquitectónicos, para formar un todo equilibrado y confortable para vivir. Al tratarse de interiores pequeños, se opta por muebles de escala reducida y colores claros, de mínimo contraste.

Los apartamentos que aquí presentamos ofrecen un amplio abanico de soluciones que se adecuan a una enorme variedad tipológica: desde pequeños estudios hasta los amplios y espaciosos *lofts*, de estética industrial, pasando por dúplex y *bungalows*, mostrando las últimas tendencias del diseño contemporáneo nacional e internacional. Numerosas ideas y estilos que constituyen una fuente de inspiración para cualquier persona interesada por el interiorismo. En definitiva, un recorrido a través de las últimas tendencias de la decoración con estilos clásicos, tradicionales, nuevos o innovadores y que no dejarán indiferentes a los amantes de la decoración.

APARTMENT IN **S'AGARÓ**

Molins Interiors // www.molinsinteriors.com

This apartment is a second home, completely open to the exterior with sea views. It is a unique, warm environment, comforted by the soft tones of the furniture, walls and upholstery. A prominent feature is the kitchen which is separated from the rest of the space through a varnished aged oak screen.

Cet appartement est une résidence secondaire complètement ouverte sur l'extérieur, avec vue sur la mer. C'est un cadre unique et chaleureux, renforcé par les tonalités du mobilier, des murs et des tissus d'ameublement. Élément caractéristique : la cuisine est séparée du reste de l'espace par un écran de vieux chêne vernissé.

Questo appartamento è abilitato come seconda casa, completamente aperto all'esteriore con vista al mare. Si tratta di uno spazio con un confort esclusivo, grazie alle tonalità morbide dell'arredamento, delle pareti e delle tappezzerie. Risalta la cucina separata dal resto mediante un *screen* in rovere verniciato effetto invecchiato.

Dieses Apartment, das als Zweitwohnung dient, öffnet sich nach außen und bietet einen herrlichen Blick auf das Meer. Die sanften Farbtöne der Möbel, Wände und Stoffe sorgen für ein warmes und einladendes Ambiente. Die Küche, die durch eine Trennwand aus gebeizter Eiche vom Rest des Apartments abgetrennt wird, sticht besonders hervor.

Dit appartement, dat een wijds uitzicht op zee biedt, is ingericht als tweede huis. De entourage is exclusief en warm, hetgeen versterkt wordt door de zachte kleurschakeringen van het meubilair, de muren en de bekleding. Opvallend is de keuken, die van de rest is afgescheiden door middel van een verouderd eikenhout gelakt *screen*.

Este apartamento, habilitado como segunda residencia, está completamente abierto al exterior para disfrutar de las vistas al mar. Resulta un entorno de exclusiva calidez, confortado por las tonalidades suaves del mobiliario, las paredes y los tapizados. Destaca la cocina separada del resto de la vivienda mediante un *screen* de roble envejecido y barnizado .

Automóvil
DE S.POL
S'AGARO

Floor plan / Grundriss / Plan
Plattegrond / Pianta / Planta

MP

APARTMENT **PORT FORUM**

Molins Interiors // www.molinsinteriors.com

The spectacular views from this home marked the arrangement of its furniture and the choice of materials and finishes. Features are the homogenous color scheme, with the predominance of white that contrast with the blue of the sea, and interesting elements such as the mirror in the dining area, which offers a reflection of the scenery to guests sitting with their backs to it.

La vue spectaculaire que l'on a depuis cet appartement a déterminé la disposition de son ameublement et le choix des matières et des finitions. Les traits dominants sont l'homogénéité du schéma chromatique, avec la prédominance du blanc qui contraste avec le bleu de la mer, et des éléments comme le miroir dans la salle à manger, qui reflète la pièce pour une partie des convives.

Lo spettacolare panorama di cui si gode da questa abitazione definisce la disposizione degli arredi, oltre che la scelta dei materiali e delle finiture. Si impongono omogeneità cromatica, in cui domina il bianco in contrasto con il blu del mare, ed elementi curiosi come lo specchio della sala da pranzo che offre il riflesso del paesaggio ai commensali seduti di spalle rispetto a questo.

Die spektakuläre Aussicht dieser Wohnung bestimmt die Anordnung des Mobiliars sowie die Wahl der Materialien und ihrer Ausführungen. Besonders hervorzuheben sind die chromatische Einheitlichkeit mit Betonung der Farbe Weiß im Kontrast zum Blau des Meeres und originelle Elemente wie der Spiegel im Esszimmer, der den Tischgästen, die mit dem Rücken zum Außenbereich sitzen, die Landschaft wiederspiegelt.

Het spectaculaire uitzicht van deze woning bepaalt de opstelling van het meubilair, alsmede de keuze van de materialen en afwerkingen. Opvallend is de chromatische homogeniteit, waarin wit in tegenstelling tot de blauwe kleur van de zee de overhand heeft, en bijzondere elementen zoals de spiegel van de eethoek, die het landschap weerspiegelt waardoor de tafelgenoten die er geen uitzicht op hebben toch van dit landschap kunnen genieten.

Las espectaculares vistas de esta residencia marcan la disposición del mobiliario, así como la elección de los materiales y los acabados. Destacan la homogeneidad cromática, en la que domina el blanco en contraste con el azul del mar, y elementos curiosos como el espejo del comedcr, que ofrece el reflejo del paisaje a los comensales que se encuentran de espaldas a él.

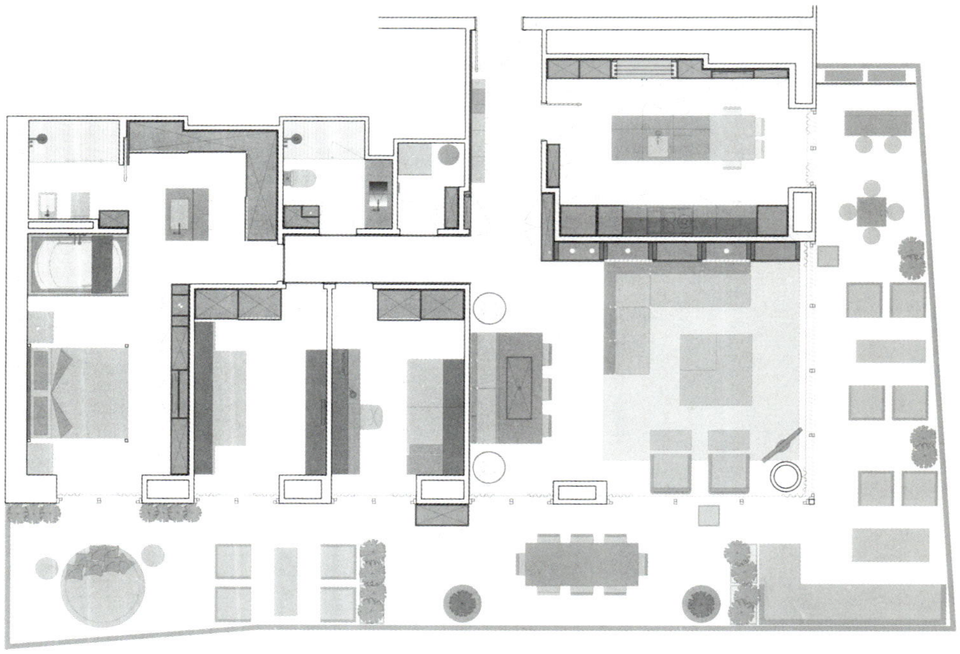

Floor plan / Grundriss / Plan
Plattegrond / Pianta / Planta

GR
GR
GR

EL ASUNTO TORNASOL
LA ESTRELLA MISTERIOSA
TINTIN AMÉRICA
TINTIN EN EL CONGO

MG

APARTMENT **JOAQUÍN COSTA**

Air Projects // www.air-projects.com

This apartment has open, light-filled and functional areas, and original features such as exposed glazed brick walls and timber beams, around which this space has been designed. The floor is a continuous surface in carriage green, a color that appears in flourishes in certain elements of the home.

Cet appartement présente des secteurs ouverts, fonctionnels et remplis de lumière, avec des traits originaux tels que des murs nus de briques vernissées et des poutres apparentes, éléments autour desquels l'espace a été conçu. Le sol est une surface continue de couleur vert wagon, qui reparaît dans certains éléments de l'aménagement intérieur.

Questo appartamento si compone di ambienti aperti e luminosi, con spazi funzionali e pratici, finiture originali della struttura come elementi verticali in mattone a vista e travicelli di legno, elemento chiave di questo spazio. Il pavimento ha un effetto continuo nei toni del verde vagone, colore che appare con pennellate su vari accessori della casa.

Diese Wohnung beherbergt klare, helle Ambiente mit funktionellen und praktischen Bereichen und origineller Ausstattung wie z. B. Wandverblendungen aus Keramikziegeln und Holzbalken, die die Schlüsselelemente dieser Räumlichkeiten darstellen. Der Bodenbelag ist durchgehend in Dunkelgrün gehalten, einer Farbe, die auch bei verschiedenen Details der Wohnung wieder aufgenommen wurde.

In dit appartement zijn veel lichte, functionele en praktische ruimten en originele afwerkingen te vinden, zoals verticale wanden van zichtbare keramische bakstenen en houten balkjes, de sleutelelementen van deze ruimte. De vloer heeft een doorlopend effect en heeft een groene kleur die hier en daar in diverse accessoires van de woning terug te vinden is.

En este apartamento se aprecian ambientes diáfanos y luminosos, con espacios funcionales y prácticos, y acabados originales de la finca, como paramentos verticales de ladrillo cerámico visto y viguetas de madera, las claves de este espacio. El pavimento es de efecto continuo en verde carruaje, un color que aparece a pinceladas en diversos accesorios de la vivienda.

MUJI

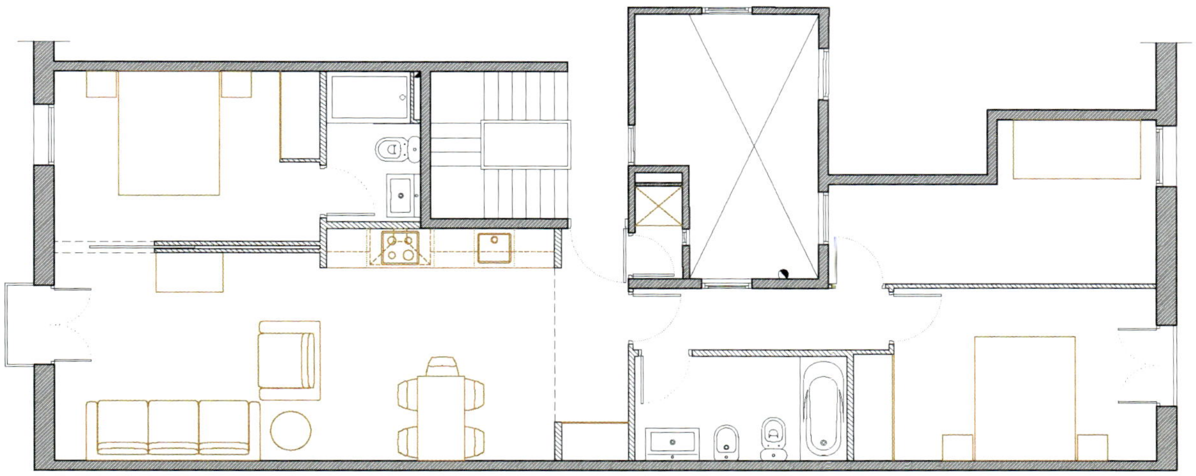

Floor plan / Grundriss / Plan
Plattegrond / Pianta / Planta

LOFT **PASSATGE DEL SUCRE (II)**

Jordi Garcés, Berta Rovira // www.jordigarces.com
Interior Design: Pia Capdevila

The combination of exposed structural elements and contemporary textures is behind the predominantly warm atmosphere of this home. The details are what enable the different spaces to offer multiple uses: a simple headboard acts as a divider between the transit area and a bedroom, while serving as the focal point of the dressing room.

La combinaison d'éléments structurels non dissimulés et de textures contemporaines est à l'origine de la chaude atmosphère de cet intérieur. Les détails permettent aux différents espaces d'offrir de multiples usages : une simple tête de lit sert de séparation entre la zone de circulation et une chambre à coucher, tout en étant le point focal du *dressing room*.

Nell'ambiente caldo di questa abitazione predomina la combinazione di elementi strutturali originali a vista con l'impiego di materiali contemporanei. Sono i dettagli a far sì che i vari spazi offrano usi molteplici: una semplice testata funge da divisorio tra la zona di passaggio e la camera e nel contempo riveste un ruolo centrale nel guardaroba.

Die warme Atmosphäre in diesem Zuhause wird von der Kombination sichtbarer Strukturelemente mit modernen Texturen geprägt. Besondere Details ermöglichen es, dass die verschiedenen Räume vielfältigen Verwendungszwecken dienen: Ein einfaches Bettkopfteil fungiert als Raumteiler zwischen Durchgangsbereich und Schlafzimmer und ist gleichzeitig Hauptelement des Ankleideraums.

In de gezellige sfeer van deze woning overheerst de combinatie van originele zichtbare structurele elementen met moderne texturen. Het zijn details die ervoor zorgen dat de verschillende ruimtes vele functies hebben: een eenvoudig hoofdeinde vormt de scheiding tussen de doorloopzone en de slaapkamer en fungeert tegelijkertijd als centraal element van de inloopkast.

En el ambiente cálido de esta vivienda predomina la combinación de elementos estructurales originales a la vista con texturas contemporáneas. Son los detalles los que hacen que los diferentes espacios ofrezcan múltiples usos: un simple cabecero separa la zona de paso y el dormitorio y, a su vez, funciona como elemento central del vestidor.

Berlin Interiors
London Interiors

ALL YOU
NEED IS
LOFT

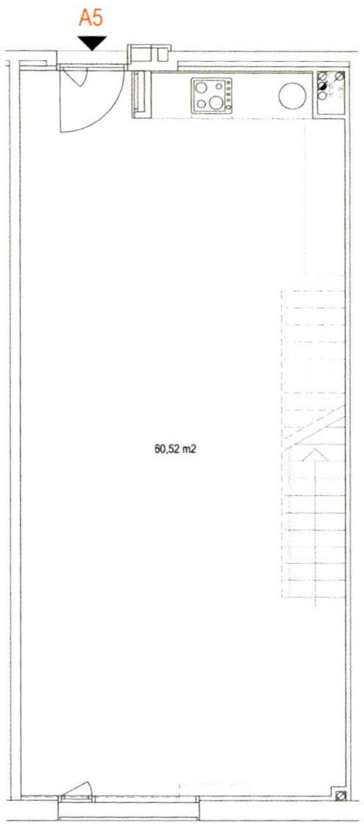

Ground floor / Erdgeschoss
Rez-de-chaussée / Begane grond
Piano terra/ Planta baja

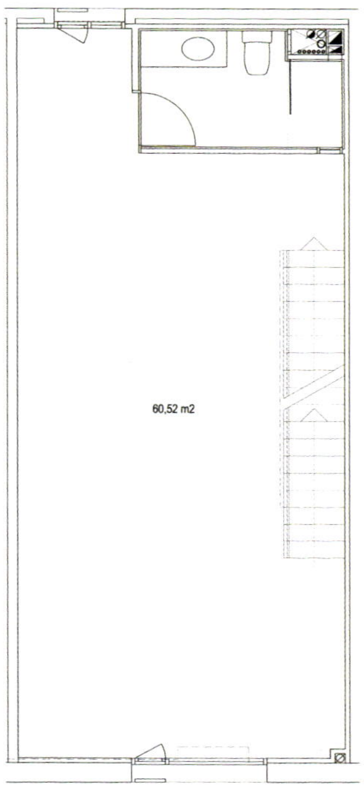

Second floor / Zweites Obergeschoss
Deuxième niveau / Tweede verdieping
Secondo piano / Segunda planta

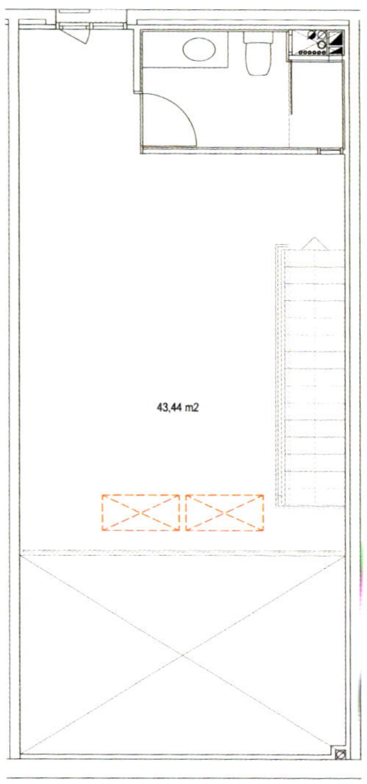

Third floor / Drittes Obergeschoss
Troisième niveau / Derde verdieping
Terzo piano / Tercera planta

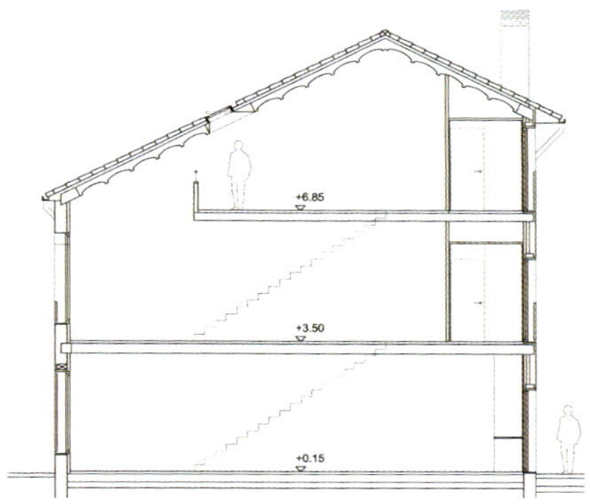

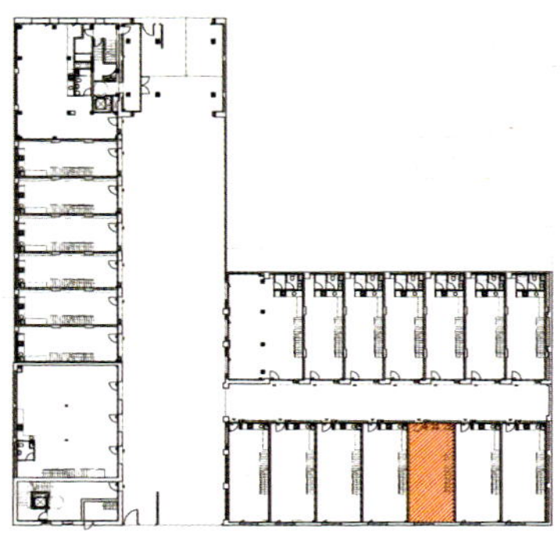

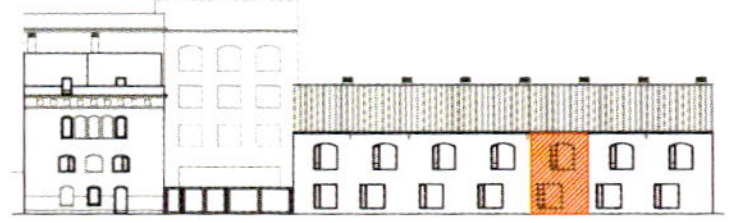

LEXINGTON
CABINS for RENT
LAKE LODGE
MALLE

THE **URBAN SUITES**

Marc Trepat, Antoni Batllori, Marta Urbiola // www.theurbansuites.com
Interior Design: Pilar Libano

These kinds of vacation apartments feature large floor-to-ceiling windows, colorful drapes, and white-walled kitchens. The contemporary open-plan spaces are meant to identify with the city of Barcelona for eminently urban guests.

Ce type d'appartement de vacances comporte généralement de grandes fenêtres de toute hauteur, des tentures colorées et des cuisines aux murs blancs. Les plans à espace ouvert sont conçus comme une signature de Barcelone, pour les hôtes urbains de qualité.

In questo tipo di appartamenti per uso turistico si impongono le enormi vetrate e il colore delle tende e delle cucine sulle pareti bianche. Si tratta di spazi luminosi di gusto contemporaneo che cercano di identificare un cliente principalmente urbano con la città di Barcellona.

Bei diesem Apartment für den touristischen Gebrauch fallen die enormen Fenster und die Farbgebung der Vorhänge und der Küche an den weißen Wänden auf. Es handelt sich um lichtdurchflutete, moderne Räume, die dem Besucher das außerordentliche Wesen der Stadt Barcelona nahe bringen sollen.

In dit soort appartementen voor toeristisch gebruik vallen de enorme ramen, de kleurengamma van de gordijnen en de keukens op witte wanden op. Het gaat om lichte ruimtes in een moderne stijl die een bij uitstek uit de stad afkomstige klant met de stad Barcelona identificeren.

En esta tipología de apartamentos para uso turístico destacan los enormes ventanales y el colorido de las cortinas y las cocinas sobre paredes blancas. Se trata de espacios diáfanos y de estilo contemporáneo que se identifican con Barcelona para atraer a clientes eminentemente urbanos.

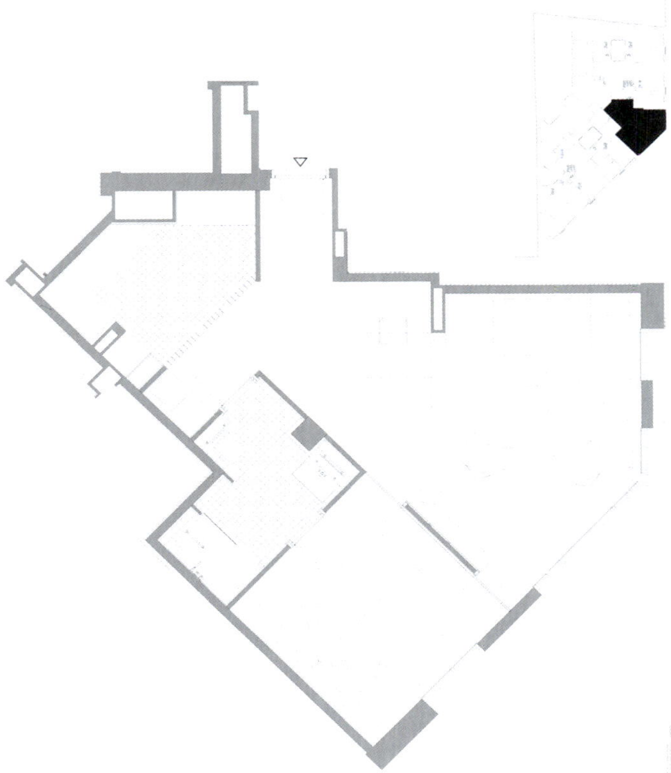

Floor plan / Grundriss / Plan
Plattegrond / Pianta / Planta

LOFT IN THE **GOTHIC**

Ingrid Matheu // www.ingridmatheu.com

This home was created from the remodeling of a suite of offices. The space is open plan with furnishings of impressive beauty and color that maintains the constant contrast of black and white. These elements are used to separate the different areas, all of which receive abundant daylight.

Cet appartement résulte du remodelage d'une suite de bureaux. L'espace est conçu en plan ouvert, avec un ameublement d'une impressionnante beauté colorée qui maintient un contraste constant entre le blanc et le noir. Ces éléments sont utilisés pour séparer les différents secteurs, tous abondamment baignés par la lumière du jour.

La ristrutturazione di un'area adibita a uffici ha portato alla creazione di questa abitazione. Si tratta di uno spazio totalmente aperto e luminoso in cui sono inseriti pezzi di grande valore estetico e cromatico, con un costante contrasto tra bianco e nero. Sono questi elementi a delimitare le varie zone, caratterizzate da una grande luminosità.

Die Restaurierung eines Bürogebäudes führte zu dieser Wohnung. Es handelt sich um einen vollkommen offenen und lichtdurchfluteten Raum, in den Möbelstücke von hohem ästhetischen und chromatischen Wert eingegliedert wurden, die einen stetigen Kontrast von Schwarz und Weiß bilden. Diese Elemente grenzen die verschiedenen, außergewöhnlich hellen Bereiche voneinander ab.

Dankzij de verbouwing van een kantoor ontstond deze woning. Het gaat om een volledig geopende en lichte ruimte waar meubels met een hoge esthetische en chromatische waarde werden gebruikt die steeds in contrast zijn met het wit en zwart. Dit zijn de elementen die de verschillende zones, die worden gekenmerkt door het vele licht, afbakenen.

La reforma ha transformado un despacho de oficinas en un loft totalmente abierto y diáfano. Destacan las piezas de mobiliario de gran valor estético y cromático, que mantienen el contraste entre el blanco y el negro. Son estos elementos los que delimitan las distintas zonas, caracterizadas por una gran luminosidad.

SAMSUNG
UN VIAJE CULINARIO

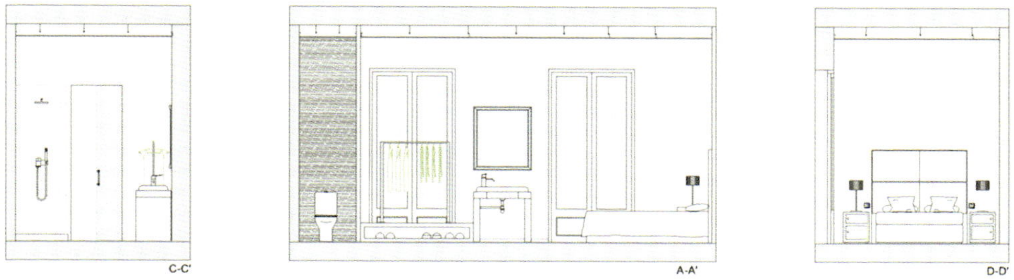

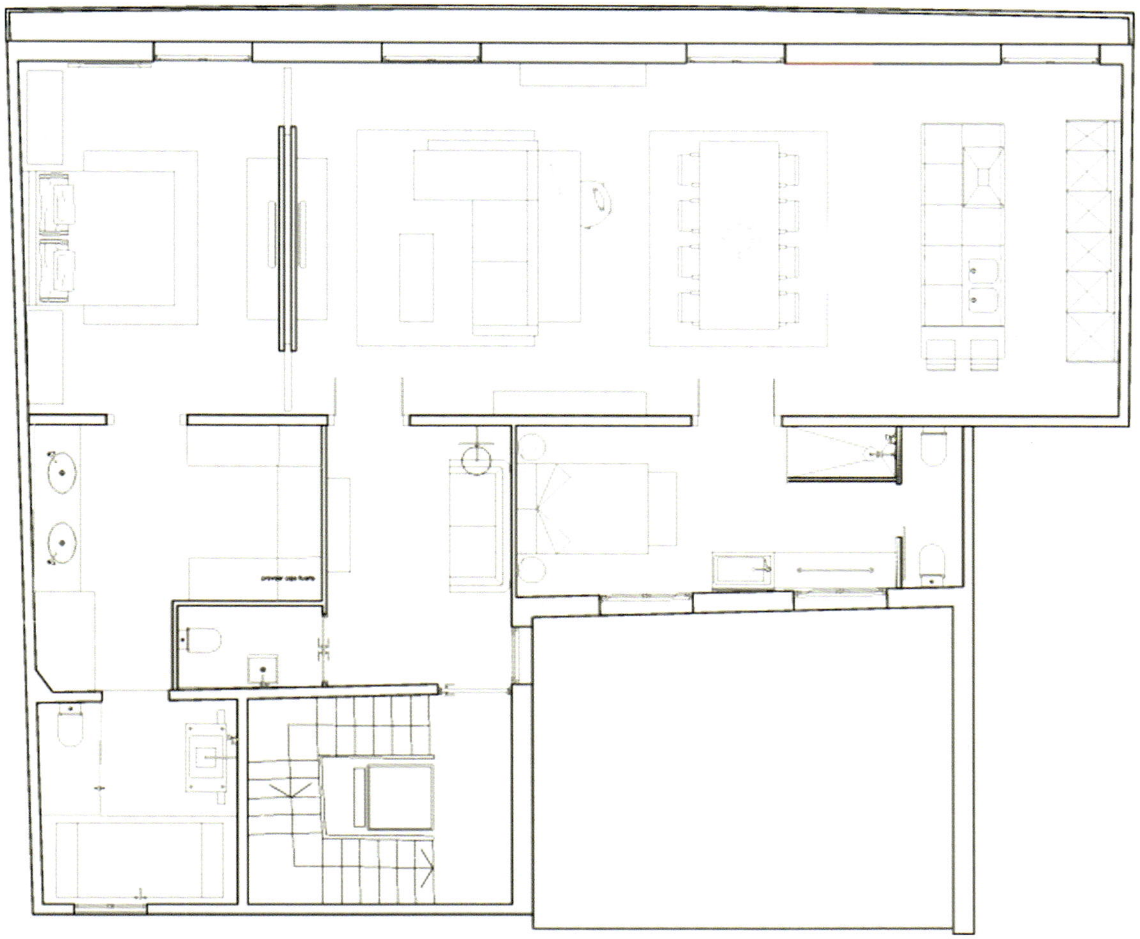

Floor plan and sections / Grundiss und Schnitte / Plan et coupes
Plattegrond en Doorsneden / Pianta e sezioni / Planta y secciones

SPRAY
ROMANICO

APARTMENT IN **NEW YORK**

James Slade, Hayes Slade / Slade Architecture // www.sladearch.com

This 430 sq ft apartment has the bed and kitchen as its basic features. The bed has folding legs and is stored in the wall behind a curtain so that the dining table can take its place. The kitchen features cabinets cut on an angle to allow light to enter from a small window located behind a column.

In diesem 40 m² großen Apartment bilden das Bett und die Küche die beiden grundlegenden Elemente. Das Klappbett versteckt sich in der Wand hinter einem Vorhang, so dass an seiner Stelle der Esstisch aufgestellt werden kann. Die Küche ihrerseits wurde mit schräg geschnittenen Schränken ausgestattet, um Licht durch ein kleines Fenster, das sich hinter einer Säule befindet, einzulassen.

Cet appartement de 40 m² est organisé autour de la table et du lit. Le lit escamotable se range dans le mur, derrière un rideau, afin que l'on puisse installer la table du repas. Les meubles de cuisine sont disposés en angle, pour permettre à la lumière de pénétrer par une petite fenêtre située derrière une petite colonne.

In dit appartement van 40 m² zijn het bed en de keuken de basiselementen. Het bed, met vouwpoten, wordt in de wand achter een gordijn verborgen om er de tafel van de eethoek voor in de plaats te zetten. De keuken is uitgerust met schuine kasten zodat er licht door het kleine raam dat zich achter een zuil bevindt naar binnen kan schijnen.

In questo appartamento di 40 m² letto e cucina sono due elementi fondamentali. Il letto, con gambe pieghevoli, si nasconde nella parete dietro una tenda per lasciare spazio al tavolo da pranzo. La cucina è stata attrezzata con pensili ad angolo che consentono il passaggio della luce da una piccola finestra ubicata dietro una colonna.

En este apartamento de 40 m² la cama y la cocina son los dos elementos básicos. La cama, con las patas plegables, se oculta en la pared tras una cortina para colocar en su lugar la mesa del comedor. Por su parte, la cocina se ha equipado con armarios cortados en ángulo para dejar pasar la luz de una pequeña ventana que se encuentra detrás de una columna.

APARTMENT IN **ABADESSA OLZET**

Rosa Rosselló // www.estudiorossello.com

Large artworks cover a large area of the walls in the living-dining room of this apartment, forming the main feature of this space. Their color and visual effect are enhanced by a black background.

Die großformatigen Kunstwerke, die einen großen Teil der Zwischenwände des Wohn- und Esszimmers bedecken, bestimmen das Bild in diesem Zuhause. Um ihre Farben und die optische Wirkung zu betonen, wurde ein schwarzer Hintergrund gewählt.

De grandes œuvres d'art couvrent de vastes sections des murs de la salle à manger de cet appartement, constituant du même coup la principale caractéristique de cet espace. Leur coloris et leur effet visuel sont mis en valeur par un fond noir.

De grote kunstwerken die een groot deel van de wanden van de woonkamer in beslag nemen, spelen een belangrijke rol. Om de kleuren ervan te accentueren en het visuele effect ervan te versterken werd een zwarte achtergrond gebruikt.

Le opere d'arte di grande formato che occupano la maggior parte delle pareti del salotto-sala da pranzo sono le grandi protagoniste. Per dare enfasi al colore e potenziare l'effetto visivo è stato creato un «telo di fondo» di colore nero.

Las obras de arte de gran formato, que ocupan buena parte de los tabiques del salón-comedor, son los grandes protagonistas de este proyecto. Para realzar su colorido y potenciar su efecto visual se han colocado sobre un fondo negro.

APARTMENT **REINA VICTORIA**

Inés Rodríguez / Air Projects // www.air-projects.com

This home occupies the two highest floors of a building located in a Barcelona suburb. The entrance hall and stairs are the focal point of the apartment, designed as a succession of common spaces – dining and living areas and study – connected by sliding doors. There is a swimming pool on the roof terrace.

Cette demeure occupe les deux étages supérieurs d'un bâtiment situé dans un faubourg de Barcelone. L'entrée et l'escalier constituent le point focal de l'appartement, conçu comme une suite d'espaces communs – salle à manger, séjour et bureau – reliés par des portes coulissantes. Il y a une piscine sur le toit en terrasse.

Questa abitazione occupa gli ultimi due piani di un edificio in un quartiere residenziale di Barcellona. L'ingresso e la scala costituiscono l'asse centrale dell'appartamento, concepito come una successione di spazi comuni - sala da pranzo, salotto e studio - uniti da porte scorrevoli. Sul tetto è stata realizzata una terrazza con piscina.

Diese Wohnung erstreckt sich über die zwei letzten Stockwerke eines Gebäudes in einem Wohnviertel von Barcelona. Der Eingangsbereich und die Treppen bilden das Rückgrat des Apartments, das als eine Folge von Gemeinschaftsräumen – Esszimmer, Wohnzimmer und Arbeitszimmer – die durch Schiebetüren verbunden sind, konzipiert wurde. Auf dem Dach wurde eine Terrasse mit Schwimmbad eingerichtet.

Deze woning neemt de twee bovenste verdiepingen van een gebouw in een luxe woonwijk in Barcelona in beslag. De hal en trap vormen de ruggengraat van het appartement, dat een opeenvolging van gemeenschappelijke ruimtes – eetkamer, living en studio – is die door schuifdeuren met elkaar zijn verbonden. De woning is voorzien van een dakterras met zwembad.

Esta vivienda ocupa las dos últimas plantas de un edificio situado en un barrio residencial de Barcelona. El vestíbulo y la escalera constituyen el eje vertebrador del apartamento, concebido como una sucesión de espacios comunes –comedor, sala de estar y estudio– unidos por puertas correderas. En la cubierta se ha dispuesto una terraza con piscina.

THE TIMES
ATLAS OF THE WORLD

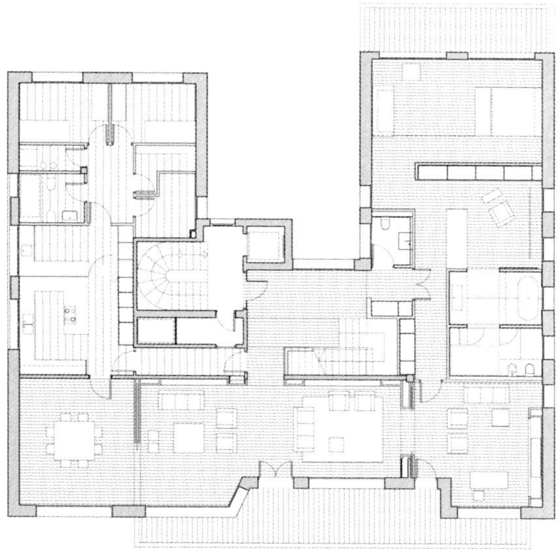

Ground floor / Erdgeschoss / Rez-de-chaussée
Begane grond / Piano terra / Planta baja

Second floor / Zweites Obergeschoss / Second niveau
Tweede verdieping / Secondo piano / Segunda planta

APARTMENT **SANT LLUÍS**

Raúl Campderrich / Air Projects // www.air-projects.com

This fully remodeled apartment has a central core that combines living and dining areas with the kitchen, achieving a homogenous dialogue between all the parts of the project. This central part also contains a small study with a large shelving unit that dominates the back wall of the space.

L'appartement entièrement remodelé possède un noyau central combinant séjour, salle à manger et cuisine, ce qui crée un dialogue homogène entre toutes les parties du programme. Cette même partie centrale accueille un petit bureau doté d'un grand ensemble de rayonnages qui domine le mur de fond de cet espace.

Appartamento completamente ristrutturato con un nucleo centrale che unisce salotto, sala da pranzo e cucina in un'unica superficie ottenendo così un dialogo omogeneo tra tutte le parti che compongono il progetto. Questa parte centrale dispone di un piccolo studio dotato di una grande scaffalatura che domina la parte finale del salotto.

In Mittelpunkt dieses vollständig renovierten Apartments steht der Kernbereich, der Wohnzimmer, Esszimmer und Küche auf einer einzigen Fläche verbindet und damit einen homogenen Dialog zwischen allen Bestandteilen des Projekts schafft. Dieser zentrale Bereich verfügt über einen kleinen Arbeitsplatz mit einem großen Bücherregal, das den Hintergrund des Raumes beherrscht.

Volledig verbouwd appartement met een centrale kern die living, eethoek en keuken in een ruimte met elkaar samenvoegt en zo een homogene dialoog ontstaat tussen de delen waaruit het project bestaat. Dit centrale deel beschikt over een kleine werkhoek voorzien van een grote boekenkast die de achterzijde van de kamer in beslag neemt.

Este apartamento completamente reformado presenta un núcleo central que aúna sala de estar, comedor y cocina en una misma superficie, consiguiendo un diálogo homogéneo entre todas las partes integrantes del proyecto. Esta zona central dispone de un pequeño estudio de trabajo dotado de una gran estantería que domina el fondo de la sala.

BARCELONA
Inglés

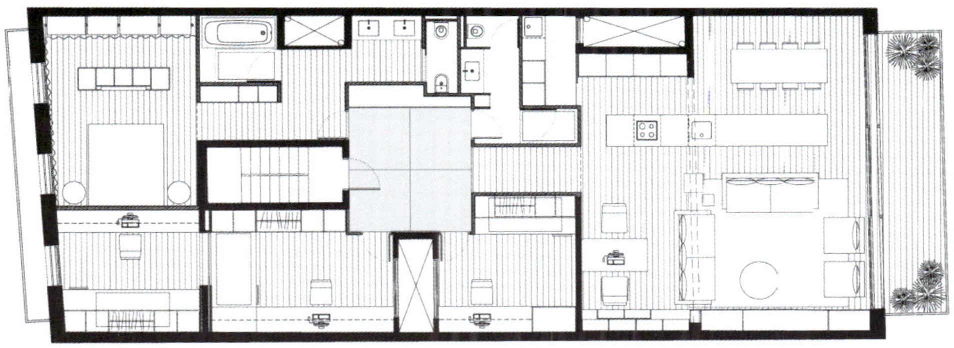

Floor plan / Grundriss / Plan
Plattegrond / Pianta / Planta

APARTMENT IN **GLOUCESTER**

Elise Ovanessoff, Stephen Quinn / Works Architecture // www.worksarchitecture.com

This apartment is the result of the remodeling of one of the floors of this hundred-year-old building to create a number of smaller dwellings. The project respected existing features, particularly the great ceiling heights, and restored the living area to its original size, making it a focal point of the space.

Cet appartement résulte du remodelage de l'un des étages d'un immeuble centenaire, pour créer plusieurs logements plus petits. Le projet a respecté les éléments préexistants, en particulier la grande hauteur sous plafond, et redonné ses dimensions au séjour pour en faire le point focal de l'espace.

Questo appartamento è il risultato della ristrutturazione di uno dei piani di un edificio secolare volta a creare nuclei abitativi di piccole dimensioni. Il progetto ha rispettato le caratteristiche preesistenti della struttura, in particolare per quanto riguarda la grande altezza dei soffitti e la restituzione delle dimensioni del salone centrale, protagonista di questo spazio.

Dieses Apartment ging aus der Renovierung einer der Etagen eines 100 Jahre alten Gebäudes hervor, durch die kleinere Wohneinheiten geschaffen werden sollten. Das Projekt berücksichtigte die vorhandenen Gegebenheiten des Anwesens (insbesondere die hohen Decken) und bewahrte die ursprüngliche Größe des zentralen Wohnzimmers, das den Hauptraum der Wohnung darstellt.

Dit appartement is het resultaat van de verbouwing van een van de verdiepingen van een eeuwenoud gebouw, waarmee men voor ogen had om kleine woningen te scheppen. Het project ging respectvol om met de vooraf bestaande waarden van het pand, in het bijzonder met de hoge wanden en met het herstel van de grootte van de centrale zitkamer die een voorname rol in de ruimte inneemt.

Este apartamento es el resultado de la reforma de una de las plantas de un edificio centenario con el fin de obtener viviendas de reducidas dimensiones. El proyecto respetó las características de la finca, en especial la gran altura de los techos, y recuperó el tamaño del salón central, que se convierte en el protagonista del espacio.

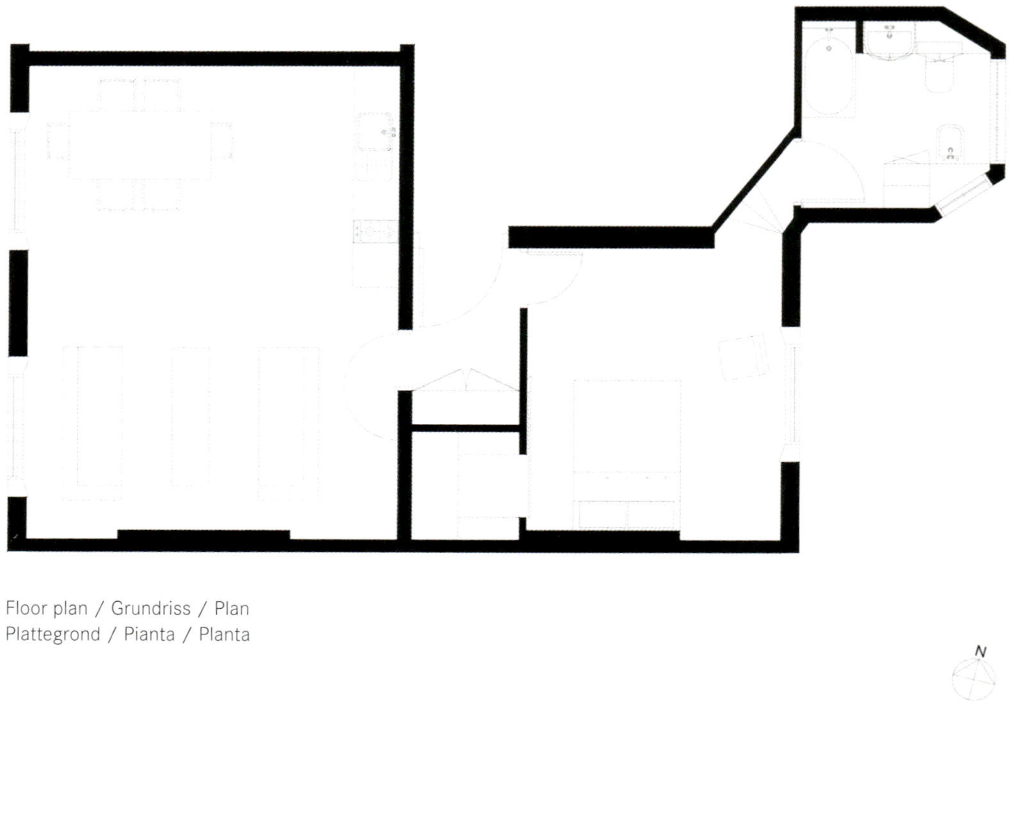

Floor plan / Grundriss / Plan
Plattegrond / Pianta / Planta

APARTMENT **CIUDAD DIAGONAL**

Ingrid Matheu // www.ingridmatheu.com

The décor, marked by a strong color scheme over a background formed by a number of the charcoal gray walls, is possible owing to the abundant daylight flooding the interior. Splashes of intense color are a feature of the different spaces, seen in the armchairs, pictures, and cushions, among others. Nevertheless, all the colors are part of a simple scheme.

La décoration, marquée par un puissant schéma de couleurs sur un arrière-plan constitué de plusieurs murs gris anthracite, est rendue possible grâce à l'abondante lumière qui baigne l'intérieur. Des taches de couleur intense distinguent les différents espaces dans les fauteuils, les tableaux et les coussins, entre autres. Toutes les couleurs s'intègrent néanmoins dans un schéma d'ensemble simple.

L'ingresso di abbondante luce naturale all'interno dell'abitazione consente la scelta di questi arredi, caratterizzati da un marcato cromatismo, che si concretizza nel colore grigio antracite di alcune pareti. Le note di colori intensi percorrono i vari spazi popolando poltrone, quadri, cuscini... Tuttavia tutti i colori sono vincolati e seguono un semplice filo argomentale.

Der starke Einfall von Tageslicht in das Innere ermöglicht diese Raumgestaltung, die durch eine markante Farbgebung – insbesondere durch das Anthrazitgrau einiger Wände – geprägt ist. Die kräftigen Farben von Sesseln, Bildern, Kissen usw. beleben die verschiedenen Räume. Alle verwendeten Farben sind jedoch gekonnt miteinander verknüpft und folgen einer bestimmten Linie.

Dankzij de massieve natuurlijke lichtinval in het interieur is deze inrichting, bepaald door een uitgesproken kleurenselectie, in concreto het antracietgrijs van een aantal wanden, mogelijk. Diepe kleuren zijn verdeeld over de diverse ruimten te vinden in de fauteuils, schilderijen, kussens, enz. Echter, alle kleuren zijn aan elkaar gekoppeld en volgen een eenvoudige leidraad.

La decoración de esta vivienda, marcada por un fuerte colorido sobre el fondo gris antracita de algunas paredes, es posible gracias a la abundante luz natural que penetra en el interior. Pinceladas de colores intensos –en las butacas, los cuadros, los cojines, etc.– salpican los diversos espacios. No obstante, todos los colores se integran armoniosamente en un esquema simple.

mosaico de ideas
EL MAR

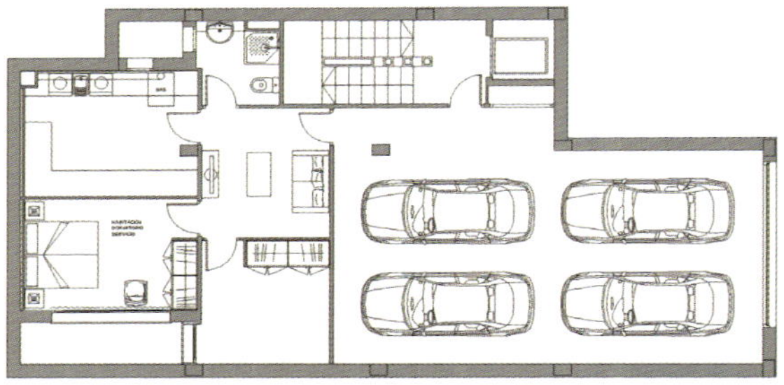

Ground floor / Erdgeschoss / Rez-de-chaussée
Begane grond / Piano terra / Planta baja

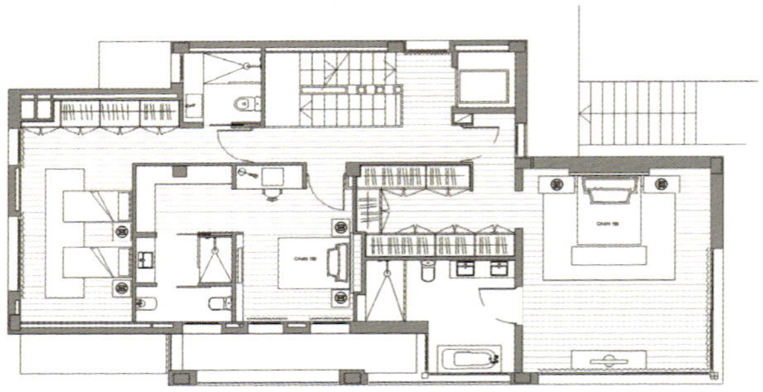

Second floor / Zweites Obergeschoss / Deuxième niveau
Tweede verdieping / Secondo piano / Segunda planta

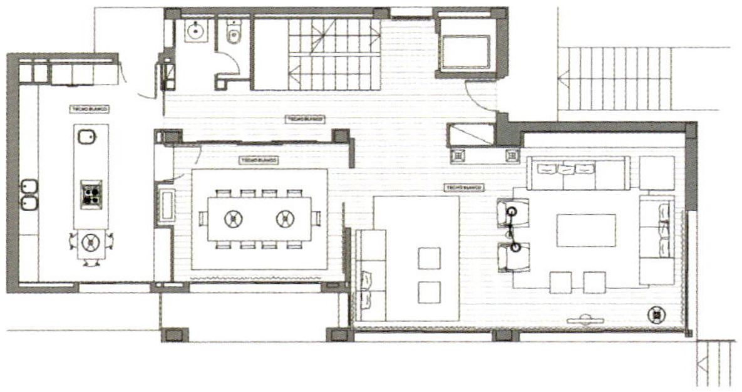

Third floor / Drittes Obergeschoss / Troisième niveau
Derde verdieping / Terzo piano / Tercera planta

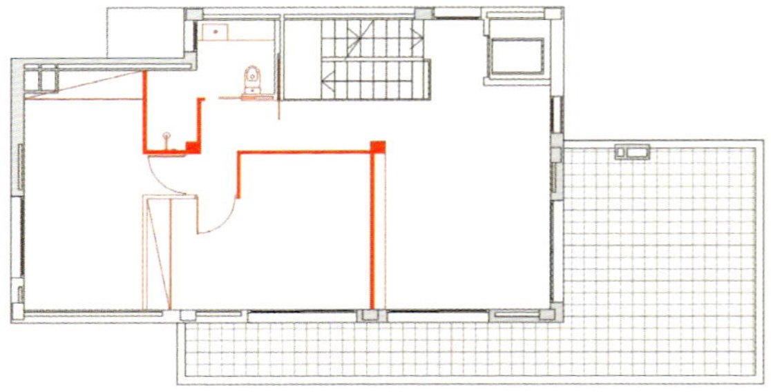

Fourth floor / Vierten Obergeschoss / Quatrième niveau
Vierde verdieping / Quarto piano / Cuarta planta

Toys for Boys

APARTMENT **SANT JUST BACH**

Joan Bach // joan.bach@coac.net

This cozy apartment has many accessories and details that give it more personality, such as the handcrafted lamp in the dining tables or the paintings decorating the walls. Finally, an old silver wall matches the upholstery of the sofa, and the sucupira wood flooring. The chimney with clean lines, represents a subtle expression to start the fire.

Cet appartement accueillant a de nombreux accessoires et détails qui lui confèrent davantage de personnalité, par exemple une lampe artisanale sur la table du repas, ou des tableaux décorant les murs. Pour finir, un mur de couleur vieil argent fait écho à la garniture du canapé et au sol en bois de sucupira. La cheminée, avec ses lignes claires, représente une subtile métaphore du feu.

Questo accogliente appartamento presenta numerosi accessori e dettagli che gli conferiscono una grande personalità, come la lampada artigianale della sala da pranzo o i quadri che decorano le pareti. Per concludere, una parete in argento antico, abbinata alla tappezzeria del sofà, e il pavimento in legname di Sucupira. La ciminiera, dalle linee depurate, rappresenta l'espressione più semplice per accendere il fuoco.

Diese einladende Wohnung wartet mit zahlreichen Accessoires und Details auf, die ihr einen eigenen Charakter verleihen, wie zum Beispiel die handgefertigte Lampe im Esszimmer oder die Bilder an den Wänden. Besondere Aufmerksamkeit ziehen die auf das Sofa abgestimmte Wand in der Farbe Altsilber und der Boden aus dem Holz des südamerikanischen Sucupira-Baumes auf sich. Der Kamin mit seinen klaren Linien ist minimalistisch gestaltet.

Dit warme appartement heeft talrijke accessoires en details die het persoonlijk maken, zoals de ambachtelijke lamp in de eetkamer of de schilderijen aan de muren. Tenslotte heeft het een muur in oud zilver die past bij de bankbekleding en de vloer van sucupira hout. De open haard met zijn verfijnde lijnen is de minimale uiting van het aanmaken van vuur.

Este cálido apartamento presenta numerosos accesorios y detalles que lo dotan de gran personalidad, como la lámpara artesanal del comedor o los cuadros que visten las paredes. Como colofón, una pared de plata vieja, a juego con el tapizado del sofá, y el suelo de madera de sucupira. La chimenea, de líneas depuradas, se reduce a la mínima expresión.

CASA DISEÑO
E INTERIORISMO

SAVON
LIQUIDE

CASA
AFRICA

APARTMENT **RAMBLA CLAUDIO**

Cristian Hoyos

The design of this apartment gives priority to the central space that encapsulates the kitchen and living and dining areas in order to offer a spacious area for gatherings. A glass partition between the kitchen and dining area provides visibility and interaction between the two spaces.

La conception de cet appartement donne la priorité à l'espace central qui intègre cuisine, salle à manger et séjour, afin d'offrir de spacieux dégagements pour les réceptions. Une cloison de verre entre la cuisine et la salle à manger assure visibilité et interaction entre ces deux espaces.

In questo appartamento è stata data priorità allo spazio centrale che comprende cucina, salotto e sala da pranzo, con l'obiettivo di disporre di un'ampia zona sociale. Tra cucina e sala da pranzo è stato inserito un divisorio di vetro che lascia visibilità e consente l'interazione tra le due zone.

In diesem Apartment wurde der Schwerpunkt auf den zentralen Raum mit Küche, Wohn- und Esszimmer gelegt, der einen geräumiger Bereich für Zusammenkünfte bietet. Zwischen Küche und Esszimmer wurde ein durchsichtiger Wandschirm aus Glas installiert, der die Interaktion zwischen beiden Bereichen ermöglicht.

In dit appartement is de centrale ruimte met de keuken, zit- en eethoek, als prioriteit gesteld, zodat er veel plaats is om samen te zijn. Tussen de keuken en de eethoek is een glasscherm geïnstalleerd waardoor er zicht en interactie tussen beide zones mogelijk is.

En este apartamento se ha priorizado el espacio central, que engloba cocina, salón y comedor, con el objetivo de disponer de una amplia zona de reunión. Entre la cocina y el comedor se ha instalado una mampara de cristal que permite la visibilidad y la interacción entre ambas zonas.

PAISAJES DEL MUNDO

GAMMEL DANSK
Campbell's
HEINZ
BAKED
BEANS

APARTMENT IN THE **CENTRE OF VALLADOLID**

Juan Luis de Madariaga // www.demadariaga.com

This apartment is located in a heritage building, the reason for which a number of existing elements were preserved, such as openings on the façade and original structural features. A careful study was made for the positioning of artificial light fixtures given that barely any daylight enters.

Cet appartement est situé dans un bâtiment historique, ce pourquoi plusieurs éléments préexistants ont été préservés comme les percées en façade et les structures d'origine. On a fait une étude très soigneuse pour le positionnement des points de lumière artificielle, étant donné la raréfaction de l'éclairage naturel.

Questo appartamento si trova in un edificio di interesse storico-artistico, per questo sono stati mantenuti gli elementi preesistenti come le aperture in facciata o i componenti strutturali originari. È stata studiata minuziosamente l'applicazione dei punti di illuminazione artificiale dato che la luce naturale è quasi assente.

Diese Wohnung befindet sich in einem denkmalgeschützten Gebäude, weshalb die Öffnungen in der Fassade und ursprünglich vorhandene Strukturelemente beibehalten wurden. Die verschiedenen Leuchtkörper wurden sehr überlegt angebracht, da kaum natürliches Licht einfällt.

Dit appartement bevindt zich in een gebouw dat onder monumentenzorg valt. Vandaar dat de vooraf bestaande elementen zoals de gaten in de gevel of de oorspronkelijke structurele componenten bewaard zijn gebleven. De plaatsen waar de kunstlichtpunten zijn geïnstalleerd zijn minutieus bestudeerd, aangezien er nauwelijks daglicht naar binnen schijnt.

Este apartamento está situado en un edificio catalogado, por lo que se han mantenido algunos elementos originales, como los huecos que había en la fachada o los componentes estructurales. Se ha estudiado minuciosamente la aplicación de los puntos de iluminación artificial, ya que apenas hay entrada de luz natural.

WON'T YOU PLEASE
PLEASE HELP ME ?

VAIO

ducha

APARTMENT **PASSEIG TAULAT**

La Maison de l'Élephant // www.lamaisondelelephant.com

The boundaries between interior and exterior are blurred in this apartment, which features a wide range of materials and finishes, together with furniture and sculpture. Among these are reproductions of terracotta warriors and a sculpture from Indonesia made from solid wood with a chrome-plated metal base.

Les limites entre l'intérieur et l'extérieur sont effacées dans cet appartement qui présente une vaste gamme de matières et de finitions, de mobiliers et de sculptures. On remarque parmi celles-ci des reproductions de guerriers en terre cuite et une sculpture indonésienne en bois massif montée sur une base métallique chromée.

In questo appartamento, dove l'esterno si fonde con l'interno, si impone la miscela di materiali e finiture diversi, cui si aggiungono elementi di arredo e sculture. Tra queste notiamo le figure di guerrieri di terracotta e un pezzo realizzato in legno massello tropicale con base in metallo cromato, proveniente dall'Indonesia.

In dieses Apartment, in dem Außen- und Innenbereiche miteinander verschmelzen, fallen die große Palette an verwendeten Materialien und Ausführungen sowie die Kombination von Möbelstücken und Skulpturen auf. Besonders hervorzuheben sind die Figuren zweier Terrakotta-Krieger und ein aus Indonesien stammendes Dekoelement aus tropischem Massivholz mit verchromten Metallfuß.

In dit appartement, waar buiten en binnen met elkaar samensmelten, vallen de combinatie van vele soorten materialen en afwerkingen op, maar ook de meubels en sculpturen. Daarvan nemen de terracotta soldatenbeeldjes en een houtsnijwerk van massief tropisch hout met een verchroomd metalen poot uit Indonesië een opvallende plaats in.

En este apartamento, en el que el exterior se funde con el interior, destaca la mezcla de una amplia gama de materiales y acabados, así como de elementos de mobiliario y esculturas. Entre ellas hay unas figuras de los guerreros de terracota y una escultura de madera tropical maciza con pie de metal cromado, procedente de Indonesia.

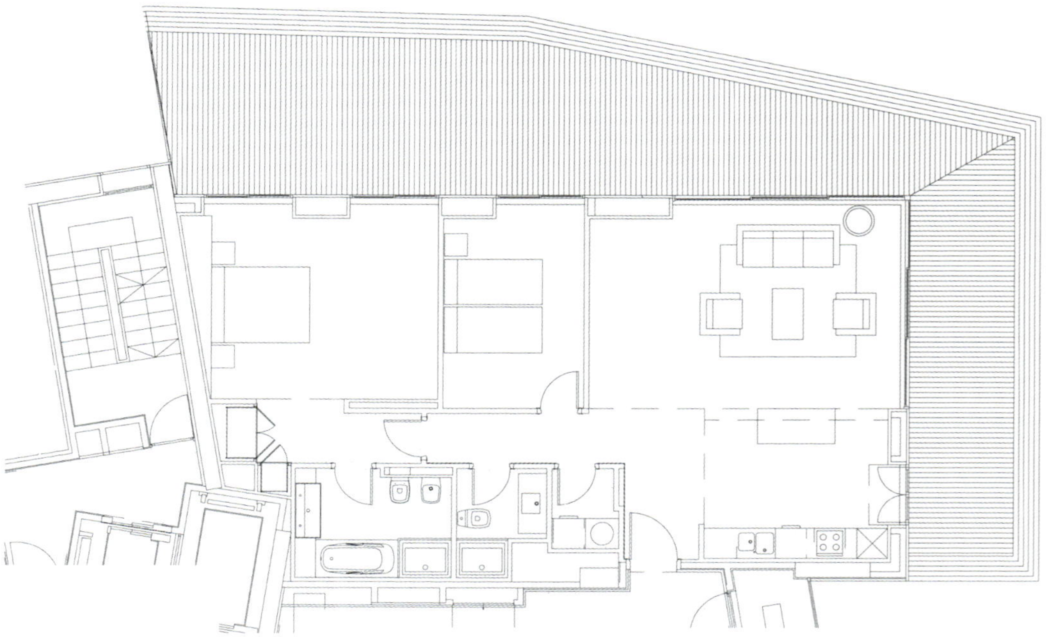

Floor plan / Grundriss / Plan
Plattegrond / Pianta / Planta

PENTHOUSE **GRAN DE GRÀCIA**

Joan Bach // joan.bach@coac.net

This spacious apartment has an innovative design as regards the combination of furniture and colors, determined by the high contrast of the painted walls against the monochromatic living room and kitchen – a space defined by the warmth of the wood and in which a sofa in dark tones stands out as a prominent feature.

Ce spacieux appartement est conçu de façon novatrice pour la combinaison du mobilier et des couleurs, déterminée par le fort contraste entre les murs peints et le monochromatisme des mobiliers du séjour et de la cuisine – espace défini par la chaleur du bois, où un canapé dans un ton sombre reste le trait dominant.

Questo spazioso appartamento ha un design innovatore conferitogli dall'incrocio dei mobili e dei colori, con un elevato contrasto sulle pareti dipinte rispetto al monocromatismo del salone-sala da pranzo e cucina, spazio marcato dal calore del legno e dal protagonismo di un sofà in toni scuri.

Diese große Wohnung besticht durch ihr innovatives Design und die besondere Mischung von Möbeln und Farben. Der Charakter dieses Zuhauses wird geprägt vom starken Kontrast zwischen den in kräftigen Farben gehaltenen Wänden und der monochromatischen Gestaltung des Wohn- und Esszimmers mit Küche, das von der Wärme des Holzes und dem Sofa in dunklen Tönen bestimmt wird.

Dit riante appartement heeft een innoverend design voor wat betreft de mengeling van meubilair en kleuren, die bepaald wordt door een sterk contrast tussen de geverfde muren en de eenkleurige zit- en eetkamer en keuken, een ruimte die gekenmerkt wordt door de warmte van het hout en een centraal staande bank in een donkere tint.

Este espacioso apartamento tiene un diseño innovador en cuanto a la mezcla de mobiliario y color. Destaca un fuerte contraste entre las paredes de vivos colores y el monocromatismo del salón-comedor y la cocina, un espacio marcado por la calidez de la madera y el protagonismo de un sofá de tonos oscuros.

APARTMENT **PORT GRAN**

Ruiz Narvaiza Associats // www.elenaruiz.com

The color white invades every corner of this house, with careful proportions and a very clean design. The space, with small dimensions and completely flooded with natural light, features a bedroom with en-suite, sharing a colored leather partition wall that gives a touch of color to the sleeping area.

La couleur blanche est omniprésente dans tous les coins de l'habitat, accompagnant le soin extrême apporté aux proportions et la grande netteté du concept. L'espace, de petites dimensions et complètement baigné de lumière naturelle, comprend une chambre à coucher avec salle d'eau attenante, séparée par un écran de cuir teinté qui donne une touche de couleur à l'ensemble.

Il colore bianco invade tutti gli angoli di questa casa, di attente proporzioni e un design molto nitido. Lo spazio, di ridotte dimensioni e completamente inondato di luce naturale, incorpora una camera da letto con bagno integrato, con un divisorio in tappezzeria nautica che dà una nota di colore alla zona notte.

Die Farbe Weiß durchdringt jeden Winkel dieser gut proportionierten Wohnung mit klaren Linien. Das kleine, jedoch sehr helle Apartment verfügt über ein Schlafzimmer mit integriertem Bad. Dieses ist durch eine mit synthetischem Leder bespannte Wand abgetrennt, welche einen Farbtupfer im Schlafbereich darstellt.

De kleur wit vult alle hoeken van deze woning, met uitgekiende proporties en een zuiver ontwerp. De ruimte, met geringe afmetingen, wordt helemaal overstroomd met hemellicht en omvat een slaapkamer met ingebouwde badkamer met een tussenmuur van nautic leather die het slaapvertrek een kleurig tintje geeft.

El color blanco invade todos los rincones de esta vivienda, que se caracteriza por unas cuidadas proporciones y un diseño muy limpio. El espacio, de reducidas dimensiones y completamente inundado de luz natural, incorpora un dormitorio con baño integrado, separados por un tabique de piel náutica que da la nota de color a la zona de noche.

BOSS

APARTMENT IN **JEREZ**

Jordi Galí // www.jgaliestudi.com

Wood is the main feature of this 1,614 sq ft home. The intention of imbuing the home with great warmth is achieved through the use of the appropriate textiles, soft lighting, wide spaces (particularly in the living and dining areas) and a rational layout of the different areas.

Le bois est l'élément principal de cet appartement de 150 m². La volonté de donner à cet intérieur une grande chaleur est réalisée par la combinaison de tissus appropriés, d'un éclairage doux, de vastes espaces (en particulier dans le séjour et la salle à manger) et d'une répartition rationnelle des différents secteurs.

Il legno è il grande protagonista di questa abitazione di 150 m². L'obiettivo di ottenere spazi molto accoglienti è potenziato dall'uso di tessuti adeguati, un'illuminazione tenue e seducente, spazi ampi (soprattutto in salotto e in sala da pranzo) e una distribuzione razionale delle diverse zone.

Holz spielt die Hauptrolle in dieser 150 m² großen Wohnung. Die Zielsetzung, Räume mit warmem Ambiente zu schaffen, wird durch den Einsatz entsprechender Textilien, eine gedämpfte und verführerische Beleuchtung, große Räume (insbesondere Wohnzimmer und Essbereich) und eine rationelle Aufteilung der verschiedenen Bereiche erfüllt.

Het hout speelt een belangrijke rol in deze woning van 150 m². Het doel om gezellige ruimten te creëren wordt bereikt door het gebruik van passende stoffen, een zwakke, verleidelijke verlichting, grote ruimtes (in het bijzonder in de zit- en eethoek) en een weloverwogen verdeling van de verschillende zones.

La madera es la gran protagonista de esta vivienda de 150 m². Se ha logrado configurar un apartamento cálido y acogedor gracias al uso de los textiles apropiados, una iluminación tenue y seductora, espacios amplios (especialmente en el salón y en el comedor) y una distribución racional de las diferentes zonas.

CHICAGO ARCHITECTURE AND DESIGN
Modernism Rediscovered
HOUSES
CASAS
HÄUSER
NEW GENERATION HOUSES
CASAS DE NUEVA GENERACIÓN

APARTMENT **EIXAMPLE**

Heres Arquitectura // www.heresarquitectura.es
Toolstudio
Interior Design: Zona Barcelona

Located in a privileged part of the Eixample district of Barcelona, this apartment underwent a total remodeling in order to give it more light and a feel of space through a more rational layout of the interior areas. The design retained original features such as the exposed ceiling beams and the tiled vaulting.

Situé dans un secteur privilégié du quartier d'Eixample à Barcelone, cet appartement a connu un remodelage complet afin de lui donner davantage de lumière et une meilleure impression d'espace grâce à une distribution plus rationnelle des zones intérieures. Le concepteur a gardé des éléments d'origine tels que les poutres apparentes du plafond et les voûtes carrelées.

Ubicato in una zona privilegiata del Eixample di Barcellona, questo appartamento è stato oggetto di una ristrutturazione totale con l'obiettivo di guadagnare luce e ampiezza spaziale partendo da una distribuzione più razionale degli spazi interni. Il progetto ha mantenuto gli elementi originali della struttura come il solaio a vista e la volta in cotto.

Dieses Apartment in einem prächtigen Anwesen im Viertel Ensanche von Barcelona wurde einer vollständigen Renovierung unterzogen, um durch eine rationellere Aufteilung des Innenraums mehr Helligkeit und einen Eindruck von Weiträumigkeit zu gewinnen. Bei dem Projekt wurden ursprüngliche Elemente des Anwesens wie z. B. schmiedeeiserne Details und Tonziegel erhalten.

Dit appartement, dat is gevestigd in een herenhuis in de Barcelonese wijk Eixample, is volledig verbouwd met als doel voor meer licht en een gevoel van ruimte te zorgen door een weloverwogen indeling van het interieur. Het project heeft oorspronkelijke elementen van het pand gespaard, zoals het zichtbare latwerk en de aardewerken overwelving van het plafond.

Situado en una finca regia del Eixample barcelonés, este apartamento ha sido objeto de una rehabilitación total con el objetivo de ganar luz y amplitud a partir de una distribución más racional del espacio interior. El proyecto ha mantenido elementos originales de la finca, como el forjado a la vista y el revoltón cerámico.

wallpaper*

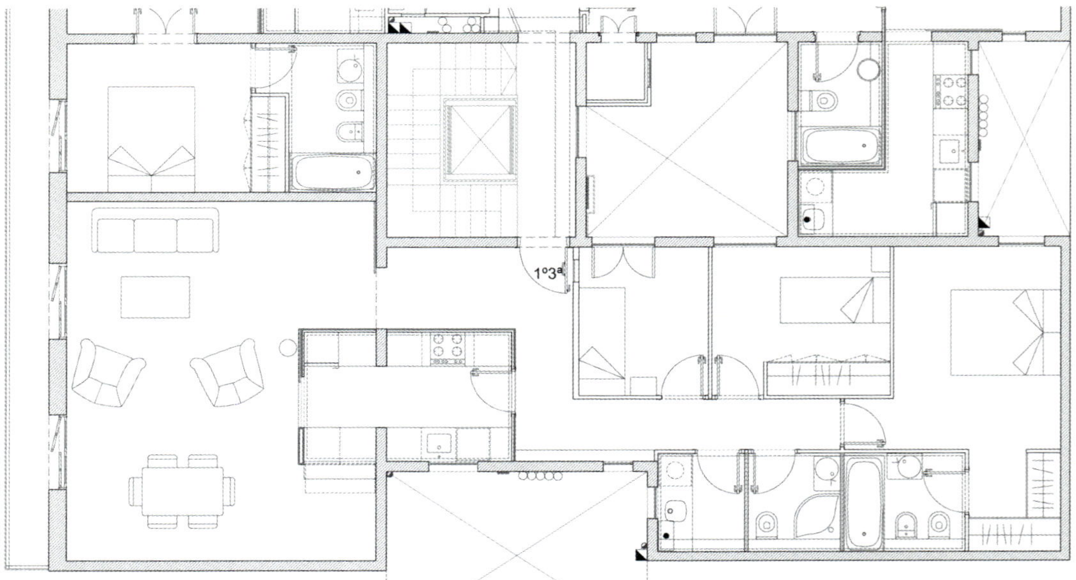

Floor plan / Grundriss / Plan
Plattegrond / Pianta / Planta

New York 1960
Toys for Boys
SERT
Geographica
SIEFF

APARTMENT IN **ROSES**

Ruiz Narvaiza Associats // www.elenaruiz.com

This home is laid out over four levels: basement, first floor, second floor (entrance), and attic. The first floor contains the sleeping areas, while the second floor houses the common areas formed by living room, dining room, and kitchen. The attic houses an open-plan space used as an artist's workshop. The underground level houses a sauna, gymnasium, and relaxation space.

Cet intérieur est aménagé sur quatre niveaux : le rez-de-chaussée, le premier étage, le deuxième étage (avec l'entrée) et le grenier. Le premier étage est celui des chambres à coucher, tandis que le second contient les espaces communs formés par le séjour, la salle à manger et la cuisine. Le grenier offre un espace ouvert utilisé comme atelier d'artiste. En sous-sol se trouvent un sauna, une salle de gymnastique et un espace de relaxation.

L'abitazione è distribuita su quattro piani: seminterrato, piano terra, primo piano (ingresso) e attico. Al piano terra si trova la zona notte mentre il primo piano ospita la zona giorno con salotto, sala da pranzo e cucina. Nell'attico troviamo una sala aperta utilizzata come studio di pittura. Infine il seminterrato ospita la sauna, la palestra e la zona relax.

Dieses Zuhause erstreckt sich über vier Stockwerke: Keller, Erdgeschoss, erster Stock (Eingang) und Dachgeschoss. Im Erdgeschoss befindet sich der Schlafbereich, während sich im ersten Stock das gesamte Tagesprogramm in Wohnzimmer, Esszimmer und Küche abspielt. Im Dachgeschoss befindet sich ein offener Raum, der als Maleratelier vorgesehen ist. Das Untergeschoss beherbergt die Sauna, den Fitnessraum und den Entspannungsbereich.

De woning is verdeeld in vier verdiepingen: souterrain, begane grond, eerste verdieping (ingang) en zolderverdieping. Op de begane grond bevindt zich de slaapzone, terwijl de eerste verdieping volledig als dagzone wordt gebruikt met een living, eethoek en keuken. De zolderverdieping beschikt over een open ruimte die wordt gebruikt als schilderatelier. Ten slotte bevindt zich in het souterrain de sauna, fitnessruimte en ontspanningszone.

La vivienda se distribuye en cuatro plantas: sótano, planta baja, primer piso (acceso) y ático. En la planta baja se ubica la zona de noche, mientras que en el primer piso se encuentra el área de día con salón, comedor y cocina. En el ático hay una sala abierta destinada a taller de pintura. Finalmente, el nivel subterráneo alberga la sauna, el gimnasio y la zona de relax.

EUROPA DESDE EL AIRE

EUROPA
DIDAC

BLACK

HOUSE IN **ALTAFULLA**

Xavier Martín // www.xaviermartin.net

Natural colors and textures prevail in this home, bringing uniformity to the combination of traditional and modern elements. The home is laid out over different levels: the dining area is a few feet below the living area and is connected to the kitchen by a sliding door.

Couleurs et textures naturelles prévalent dans cet appartement, en apportant une certaine cohérence à la combinaison d'éléments traditionnels et modernes. L'appartement est disposé sur plusieurs niveaux : la salle à manger est à quelques pieds sous le séjour et elle est connectée à la cuisine par une porte coulissante.

In questa casa dominano materiali e colori naturali, che creano omogeneità cromatica, e la combinazione di elementi tradizionali e moderni. La casa è distribuita su vari livelli: la sala da pranzo si trova alcuni metri sotto il salotto e comunica con la cucina tramite una porta scorrevole.

In dieser Wohnung herrschen natürliche Materialien und Farben, die eine farbliche Homogenität schaffen, sowie die gekonnte Kombination traditioneller und moderner Elemente vor. Das Zuhause ist in unterschiedliche Ebenen aufgeteilt: Das Esszimmer befindet sich ein paar Meter unterhalb des Wohnzimmers und bietet durch eine Schiebetür Zugang zur Küche.

In deze woning overheersen natuurlijke texturen en kleuren, die voor een chromatische homogeniteit zorgen, en de combinatie van traditionele en moderne elementen. Het huis is verdeeld in verschillende hoogtes: de eethoek ligt een paar meter onder de zithoek en wordt door middel van een schuifdeur met de keuken verbonden.

En esta vivienda dominan las texturas y los colores naturales, que aportan homogeneidad cromática, y la combinación de elementos tradicionales y modernos. La casa se distribuye en diferentes niveles: el comedor se sitúa unos metros por debajo del salón y se comunica con la cocina mediante una puerta corredera.

D
J
DJ

APARTMENT **J.G.**

Jordi Galí // www.jgaliestudi.com

The kitchen is the focal point of this project. Separated from the rest of the space by a sliding door, it features a broad counter in stainless steel that runs the length of a wall. A bright blue glass wall produces an attractive optical effect while separating the bathroom from the bedroom.

La cuisine est le point focal de ce programme. Séparée du reste de l'espace par une porte coulissante, elle présente un large plan de travail en acier inoxydable qui occupe toute la longueur d'un mur. Une cloison de verre bleu produit un séduisant effet d'optique, tout en séparant la salle d'eau de la chambre à coucher.

La cucina è il cuore di questo progetto. Costituita da un ampio bancone di lavoro in acciaio inossidabile che si estende lungo la parete, rimane separata dal resto degli spazi tramite una porta scorrevole. Una parete in vetro blu brillante, che crea un interessante effetto ottico, funge da divisorio tra il bagno e la camera.

Die Küche mit ihrer Arbeitstheke aus Edelstahl, die sich auf der ganzen Länge der Wand erstreckt, steht im Mittelpunkt dieses Einrichtungsprojekts. Sie wird durch eine Schiebetür vom übrigen Raum getrennt. Ein Wandschirm aus glänzend blauem Glas, das einen interessanten optischen Effekt bewirkt, trennt Bad und Schlafzimmer.

De keuken is het middelpunt van dit project. De keuken, gevormd door een ruime werktafel in roestvrij staal die zich langs de hele wand uitstrekt, is gescheiden van de rest van de ruimte door een schuifdeur. Een kamerscherm van glanzend blauw glas, die een bijzonder optisch effect heeft, fungeert als scheiding tussen de bad- en de slaapkamer.

La cocina es el punto central de este proyecto. Formada por un amplio banco de trabajo en acero inoxidable que se extiende a lo largo de la pared, queda separada del resto del espacio por una puerta corredera. Una mampara de cristal azul brillante, que crea un sugerente efecto óptico, actúa como división entre el baño y el dormitorio.

APARTMENT IN **BALMES**

Molins Interiors // www.molinsinteriors.com

Wood and warm colors are the predominant features of this home, present in the matte varnished oak floors and in most of the furniture, which was custom made. A unique custom-made varnished oak desk in the living room matches the floor and has side modules for drawers and office equipment.

Le bois et les couleurs chaudes sont les caractéristiques prédominantes de cet habitat, présents dans les parquets de chêne à vernis mat et dans la plupart des meubles, faits sur mesure. Dans la salle de séjour, un buffet en chêne vernis fait écho au parquet ; il est équipé sur mesure de modules latéraux de tiroirs pour le matériel de service.

Abitazione in cui predominano il legno e i toni caldi, dal pavimento realizzato in rovere naturale con finitura satinata a gran parte degli arredi, su misura. In salotto troviamo un singolare tavolino da ufficio, anch'esso realizzato su misura in rovere verniciato che riprende il parqué e comprende moduli laterali per cassetti e attrezzature da ufficio.

In dieser Wohnung herrschen Holz und warme Töne vor, vom matt lackierten Eichenholzparkett bis zum Großteil des maßgefertigten Mobiliars. Im Wohnzimmer gibt es einen ungewöhnlichen Schreibtisch, ebenfalls aus lackiertem Eichenholz passend zum Parkett nach Maß entworfen, in den seitliche Modu e für Schubladen und Büroausstattung eingebaut sind.

Woning waarin hout en warme kleuren, in de vloer van mat gelakt natuurlijk eikenhout en de meeste op maat gemaakte meubels, een belangrijke rol spelen. In de living staat een bijzonder bureau, die ook op maat is gemaakt van gelakt eikenhout en bij het parket past, en die zijmodules met laden en kantoorapparatuur bevat.

La madera y lcs tonos cálidos –presentes tanto en el pavimento, realizado en roble natural barniz mate, como en la mayoría de las piezas del mobiliario, hechas a medida– son las principales características de esta vivienda. En el salón destaca una singular mesa de despacho, también diseñada a medida en roble barnizado a juego con el parqué, y que incorpora módulos laterales para cajones y equipamiento oficina.

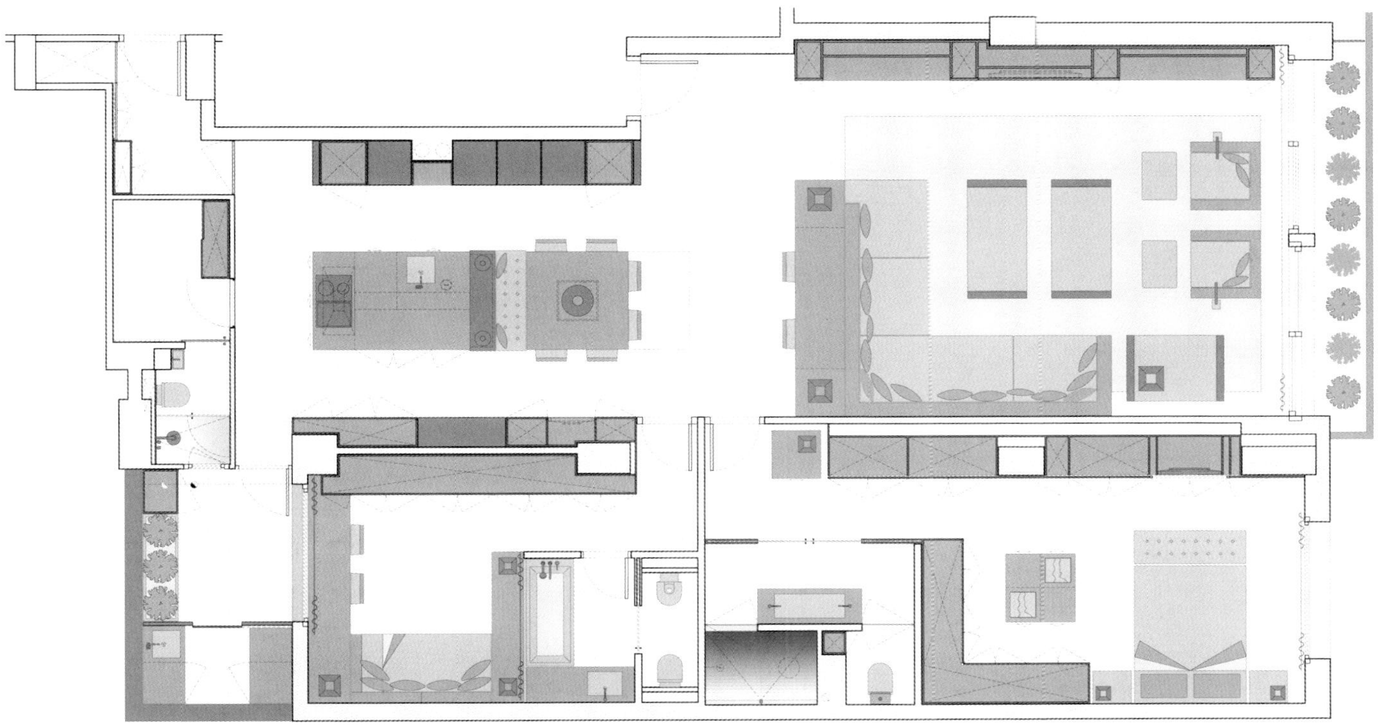

Floor plan / Grundriss / Plan
Plattegrond / Pianta / Planta

BVLGARI

LOFT **CRUSCH**

Gus Wüstemann // www.guswustemann.com

This irregularly laid out 2045 sq ft loft is located in Barcelona's Gothic Quarter. The living room brings together the identifying features of this home: Original ceilings with exposed beams and vaulting, walls in exposed brick or stone coated in clear varnish that allows fragments of also original frescoes to be seen.

Ce loft de 190 m², de plan irrégulier, est situé dans le quartier gothique de Barcelone. La salle de séjour résume bien les traits identifiant cette résidence : poutres apparentes et voûte d'origine, murs de pierres ou de briques à nu, revêtus d'un vernis clair qui laisse voir les fragments des fresques d'origine.

Nel *barrio gótico* di Barcellona troviamo questo *loft* dalla pianta eterogenea, che si sviluppa su 190 m². Nel salotto sono racchiusi gli elementi distintivi di questa abitazione: soffitti originali a piccole volte con travicelli di legno e pareti a mattoni o in pietra trattate con vernici trasparenti per lasciare in vista frammenti di affreschi, anch'essi originali.

Dieses 190 m² große Loft mit unregelmäßigem Grundriss befindet sich in der Altstadt von Barcelona. Im Wohnzimmer konzentrieren sich die Identitätsmerkmale dieser Wohnung: Originaldecken mit Holzbalkenwerk und rohe bzw. mit transparentem Lack überzogene Ziegelwände, die außerdem einige ursprüngliche Fresko-Fragmente sichtbar lassen.

In de gotische wijk van Barcelona bevindt zich deze *loft* met een heterogene vorm van 190 m². De salon bevat de onderscheidingstekens van de woning: originele plafonds met een overwelving van houten balken en ruwe wanden van transparant gelakte baksteen of steen om eveneens originele fragmenten van fresco's te onthullen.

En el barrio gótico de Barcelona se encuentra este *loft* de planta irregular de 190 m². El salón reúne las señas de identidad de la vivienda: techos originales de bovedilla con viguería de madera y paredes de ladrillo o piedra vistas barnizadas con barniz transparente que deja ver fragmentos de los frescos originales.

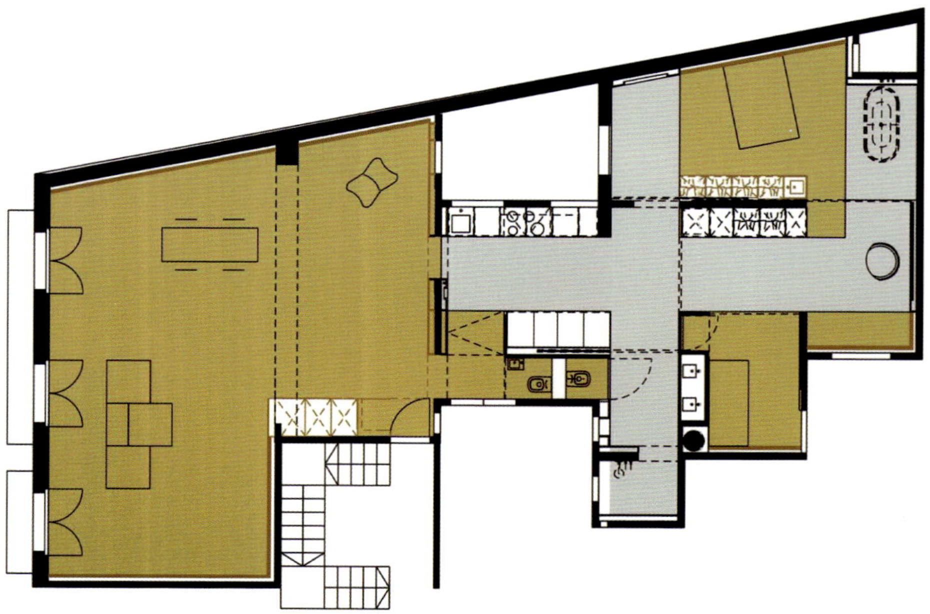

Floor plan / Grundriss / Plan
Plattegrond / Pianta / Planta

APARTMENT **VILADA**

Agustí Costa // www.agusticosta.com

The feature of the dining area in this duplex apartment is the weathered steel fireplace. This home opens to the exterior, a rural setting surrounded by medium-height mountains, and reinterprets the landscape using contemporary materials and technology.

Le trait essentiel de cet appartement en duplex est la cheminée en acier patiné. La demeure s'ouvre sur l'extérieur – un environnement rural, dans un cadre de montagnes moyennes – et elle réinterprète le paysage en utilisant les matériaux et la technologie contemporains.

In questo appartamento a due piani il protagonista della sala da pranzo è il caminetto, realizzato in acciao cor-ten. L'abitazione è collegata all'esterno, un ambiente rurale circondato da montagne di media altezza, con una reinterpretazione del luogo con materiali e tecnologie attuali.

In diesem zweigeschossigen Apartment spielt der Kamin aus Cortenstahl im Essbereich eine zentrale Rolle. Die Wohnung ist durch eine durchdachte Gestaltung mit modernen Materialien und aktueller Technologie mit der Außenwelt, einem ländlichen, von mittelhohen Bergen umgebenen Gebiet, verbunden.

In de woonkamer van dit appartement met twee verdiepingen neemt de open haard van cortenstaal een belangrijke plaats in. Deze woning is met zijn landelijke bergachtige omgeving verbonden door een reïnterpretatie van de plek met actuele materialen en technologieën.

En este apartamento de dos plantas el elemento protagonista del comedor es la chimenea de acero corten. El proyecto ha buscado abrir la vivienda al exterior, un paisaje rural de montañas medianas, llevando a cabo una reinterpretación del lugar con materiales y tecnologías actuales.

APARTMENT **COLLSEROLA**

Ujo Pallarés // www.arsspatium.com

This project involved the total remodeling of a 1,507 sq ft apartment on the slopes of Mount Collserola. The design sought to create a visual connection between the living and dining areas and the kitchen, while maintaining their separate natures. This connection was achieved with very low furniture and clear glass to compartmentalize the spaces.

Le programme impliquait le remodelage intégral d'un appartement de 140 m², sur les pentes du Mont Collserola. La conception s'est efforcée de créer une connexion visuelle entre le séjour, la salle à manger et la cuisine, tout en maintenant leur séparation. Cette connexion a été obtenue à l'aide de mobiliers très bas et de cloisons de verre clair pour compartimenter les espaces.

Ristrutturazione integrale di questo appartamento di 140 m², situato sui fianchi di Collserola. Il progetto ricerca il collegamento visivo tra salotto, sala da pranzo e cucina, rendendo nel contempo questi spazi indipendenti. Questo collegamento viene ottenuto attraverso elementi di arredo piuttosto bassi e vetri trasparenti che suddividono gli spazi.

Durch die umfassende Renovierung dieser 140 m² großen Wohnung am Collserola-Park sollten Wohnzimmer, Esszimmer und Küche visuell verbunden werden, gleichzeitig jedoch sollte die Unabhängigkeit der einzelnen Bereiche gewahrt bleiben. Diese Verbindung wird mit niedrigen Möbeln und durchsichtigem Glas für die Aufteilung erreicht.

Algehele verbouwing van dit appartement van 140 m², gelegen op de helling van de Collserola. Het project zoekt een visuele samenhang tussen de living, eethoek en keuken, maar tegelijkertijd moeten het onafhankelijke ruimtes blijven. Dit verband wordt verkregen met lage meubels en doorzichtig glas om de ruimten van elkaar te scheiden.

La reforma integral de este apartamento de 140 m², situado en la ladera de Collserola, ha buscado conectar visualmente el salón, el comedor y la cocina, que sin embargo continúan siendo espacios independientes. Esto se ha logrado mediante piezas de mobiliario de escasa altura y cristales transparentes para compartimentar los espacios.

GIORGIO BOCCA
SARFATTI
PANSA
GIORGIO BOCCA
MUSSOLINI
GARZON
VITTORIO MESSORI | OPUS DEI

salt

BISMARCK

APARTMENT **PORTA DE SARRIÀ**

GCA Arquitectes Associats // www.gcaarq.com

The interior of this apartment is minimalist, with important contrasts between the light and dark shades of materials and decorative elements. Added space comes by means of a perforated metal structure that blurs the boundaries between interior and exterior, allowing a great deal of sunlight to pass through.

L'intérieur de cet appartement est minimaliste, avec d'importants contrastes entre les teintes sombres et claires des matériaux et des éléments de décoration. L'espace additionnel provient d'une structure en métal perforé qui efface les frontières entre l'intérieur et l'extérieur, en permettant de surcroît une meilleure pénétration de la lumière du jour.

L'estetica minimalista costituisce l'essenza di questo appartamento, che propone un gioco di contrasti sobri tra toni chiari e scuri di materiali ed elementi decorativi. Si è guadagnato spazio tramite la creazione di una struttura sfumata che fonde interno ed esterno e consente il passaggio di grandi quantità di luce solare.

Minimalistische Ästhetik bestimmt das innenarchitektonische Wesen dieses Apartments, das sich in einem Spiel von nüchternen Kontrasten zwischen dunklen und hellen Tönen der Materialien und dekorativen Elemente ausdrückt. Durch eine nuancierte Struktur, die Innen und Außen verbindet und viel Sonnenlicht einlässt, wurde Platz gewonnen.

Het minimalistische aspect is de essentie van het interieur van dit appartement, dat sobere contrasten tussen de lichte en donkere kleuren van de decoratieve materialen en elementen bevat. Er is ruimte gewonnen door de creatie van een geschakeerde structuur die binnen en buiten doet samensmelten en een grote hoeveelheid zonlicht naar binnen laat schijnen.

La estética minimalista constituye la esencia de este apartamento, que propone un juego de contrastes sobrios entre tonos claros y oscuros de materiales y elementos decorativos. Se ha ganado espacio mediante la creación de una estructura matizada que fusiona interior y exterior, y permite el paso de una gran cantidad de luz solar.

APARTMENT IN THE **CENTRE OF BARCELONA**

Casamitjana // www.casamitjana.com

This restrained aspect of this apartment is the result of remodeling done to the building, which previously contained offices. The new project combines very different mater als, such as stainless steel, matte and glossy enamels, aluminum, and vinyl. The large spaces were designed with maximum functionality in mind, as required by the occupants.

L'aspect maîtrisé de cet appartement résulte du remodelage du bâtiment qui abritait auparavant des bureaux. Le nouveau programme combine diverses matières comme l'acier inoxydable, les vernis mats et brillants, l'aluminium et le vinyle. Les grands espaces ont été conçus pour assurer le maximum de fonctionnalité, conformément au désir des occupants.

Questo appartamento dall'estetica sobria è il risultato di una ristrutturazione di tutto l'edificio, precedentemente adibito a uffici. Nel nuovo progetto convivono materiali molti diversi come l'acciaio inossidabile, le laccature satinate e lucide, gli elementi in alluminio e vinile. Gli spazi, molto ampli, ricercano la massima funzionalità, secondo le necessità espresse dagli inquilini.

Dieses Apartment, das durch seine nüchterne Ästhetik besticht, ist das Ergebnis einer Renovierung des gesamten Gebäudes, in dem sich vorher Büros befanden. Bei der Gestaltung wurden unterschiedliche Materialien wie Edelstahl, matte und glänzende Lackierungen, Aluminium und Vinyl kombiniert. Bei den großen Räumen wurde der Schwerpunkt auf Wunsch der Mieter auf größtmögliche Funktionalität gelegt.

Dit sober uitziend appartement is het resultaat van een verbouwing van het hele gebouw dat voorheen werd gebruikt voor kantoren. In het nieuwe project worden zeer diverse materialen bij elkaar gevoegd, zoals roestvrij staal, matte en glanzende lak, aluminium en vinyl. De grote ruimten zoeken de door de huurders vereiste hoogste functionaliteit.

Este apartamento de estética sobria es el resultado de una reforma llevada a cabo en todo el edificio, anteriormente habilitado para oficinas. En el nuevo proyecto conviven materiales muy diversos, como el acero inoxidable, las lacas mates y con brillo, los aluminios y los vinilos. Los espacios, de grandes dimensiones, buscan la máxima funcionalidad, requerida por los inquilinos.

Cassina

APARTMENT IN **BEGUR**

Marta Cervelló

The dining area, kitchen, and library share a single space in this apartment, featuring a glazed expanse that overlooks the porch and lets daylight into this area. This common space for the home features gems of contemporary design.

La salle à manger, la cuisine et la bibliothèque partagent un seul et même espace dans cet appartement qui offre une étendue vitrifiée englobant l'entrée et permettant ainsi à la lumière de pénétrer cet espace. Cet espace commun de l'appartement offre des prémices de stylisme contemporain.

La sala da pranzo, la cucina e la biblioteca condividono un unico spazio in questo appartamento, caratterizzato da vetrate di grande impatto sul lato del porticato che consentono l'ingresso di luce naturale nella zona giorno. Questo spazio comune della casa è stato arredato con veri gioielli del design contemporaneo.

Essbereich, Küche und Bibliothek wurden in diesem Apartment in einem einzigen Raum zusammengefasst. Die Wohnung zeichnet sich durch die beeindruckenden Glaswände aus, die sie zur Veranda hin abschließen und viel Tageslicht einfallen lassen. Der Gemeinschaftsraum dieses Zuhauses wurde mit echten Kostbarkeiten des zeitgenössischen Designs ausgestattet.

De eethoek, keuken en boekenkast delen één ruimte in dit appartement dat wordt gekenmerkt door de kracht van de glazen afsluiting die uitkomt op de veranda en waardoor het natuurlijke licht naar binnen kan schijnen. Deze gemeenschappelijke ruimte is uitgerust met ware juwelen van modern design.

El comedor, la cocina y la biblioteca comparten un único espacio en este apartamento, caracterizado por el cerramiento acristalado que da hacia el porche y que permite la entrada de luz natural a esta zona de día. Este espacio común de la casa se ha equipado con auténticas joyas del diseño contemporáneo.

FRESC

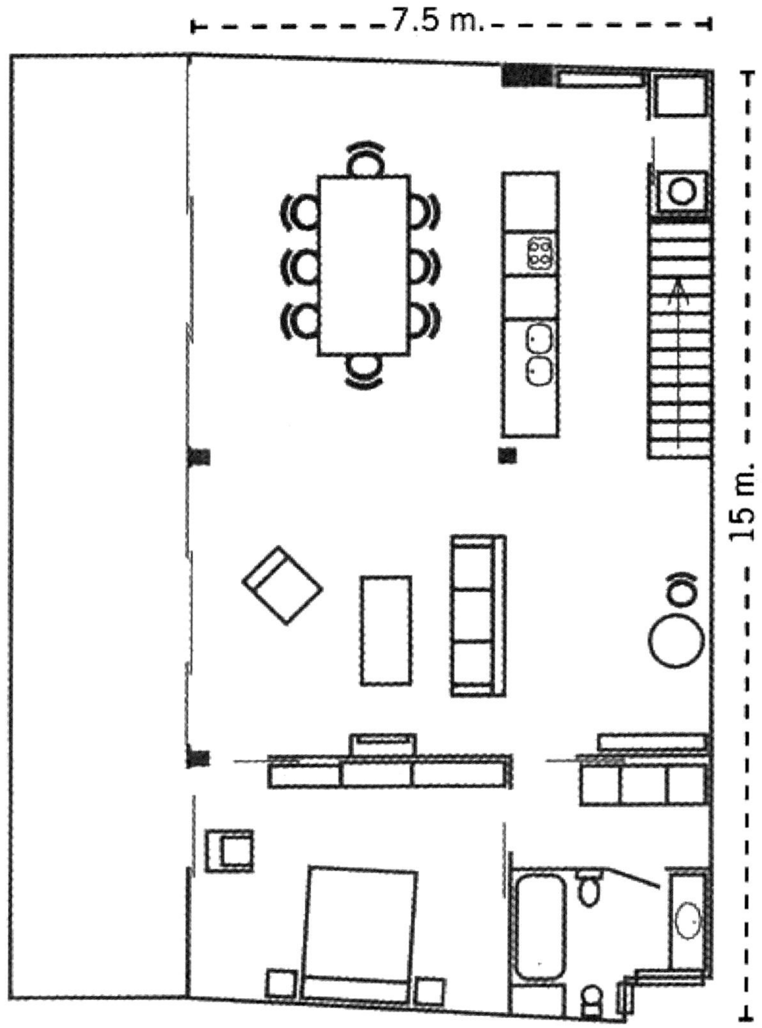

Ground floor / Erdgeschoss / Rez-de-chaussée
Begane grond / Piano terra/ Planta baja

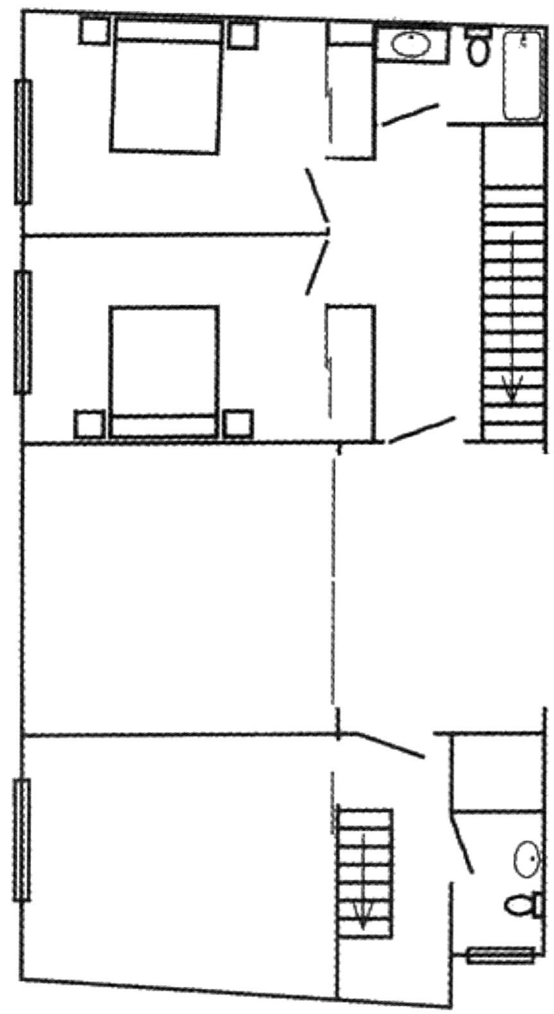

Second floor / Zweites Obergeschoss / Second niveau
Tweede verdieping / Secondo piano / Segunda planta

PEIX
PURI
FRESC

peix
puri
FRESC

APARTMENT IN **TARRAGONA**

Mantequilla Negra // mantequillanegra@tinet.org

The remodeling of a late 19th-century house gave rise to this apartment. The dining are is the focal point of the home as it connects the living area with the kitchen and an open space used for work and as a library. The original doors of carved wood have been turned into headboards, which contrast with the different fabric textures.

La restructuration d'une maison de la fin du XIXe siècle a donné naissance à cet appartement. La salle à manger est le point focal de l'intérieur, en assurant la connexion entre le séjour, la cuisine et un espace ouvert utilisé comme bureau et comme bibliothèque. Les portes d'origine en bois sculpté ont été transformées en têtes de lit, contrastant avec les différents tissus d'ameublement.

La ristrutturazione di un'abitazione di fine '800 ha portato alla realizzazione di questo appartamento. La sala da pranzo constituisce l'elemento centrale in quanto mette in comunicazione salotto, cucina, uno spazio aperto di lavoro e la biblioteca. Le porte originali si sono convertite in stupende testate di legno lavorato con finiture che contrastano con le varie finiture dei tessuti.

Durch den Umbau einer Wohnung aus der Zeit gegen Ende des 19. Jahrhunderts entstand dieses neue Zuhause. Der Essbereich bildet ein zentrales Element, da er das Wohnzimmer, die Küche und einen offenen Arbeitsplatz mit Bücherregal miteinander verbindet. Die Originaltüren wurden zu prächtigen Kopfteilen aus geschnitztem Holz umfunktioniert, die mit den verschiedenen Textilien im Schlafzimmer kontrastieren.

Dit appartement is het resultaat van de verbouwing van een woning van het eind van de 19e eeuw. De eetkamer is het centrale punt. Dit vertrek communiceert namelijk met de zitkamer, de keuken en een open werkruimte en boekenkast. De oorspronkelijke deuren zijn veranderd in mooie hoofdeinden van bewerkt hout met afwerkingen die een contrast vormen met de verschillende soorten textiel die zijn gebruikt.

Este apartamento es el resultado de la remodelación de una vivienda de finales del siglo XIX. El comedor constituye el elemento central, ya que conecta el salón, la cocina y un espacio abierto de trabajo y biblioteca. Las puertas originales se han convertido en bellos cabezales de madera labrada con acabados que contrastan con los diferentes textiles.

MEDIEVAL
TARRACO

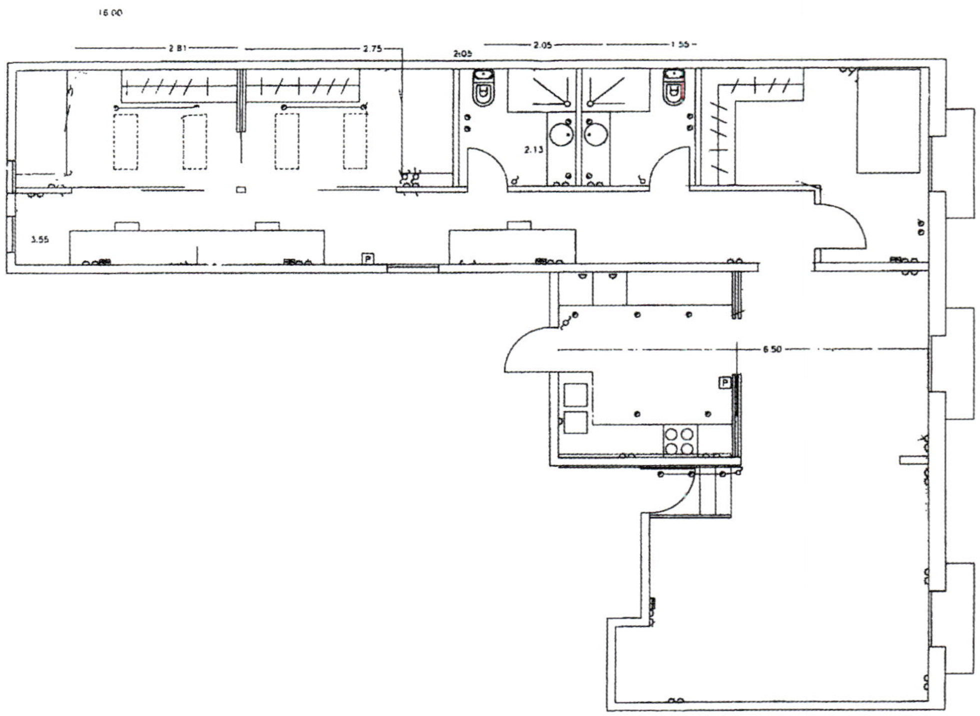

Floor plan / Grundriss / Plan
Plattegrond / Pianta / Planta

POTATO BOOK
BEAN BOOK
GREENS
The Great
CHILE POSTER

POTATO BOOK
BEAN BOOK
GREENS
The Great
CHILE POSTE

SOCIOLOGIA
Diccionari
Anglès
Català
HISTORIA DE LA BELLEZA
Webster's New World Dictionary

APARTMENT IN **GRÀCIA**

Jordi Queralt // www.jordiqueralt.com

Except for the sleeping areas, the rooms of this single-floor apartment are interconnected both in structure and in aspect. The dining area becomes a central node between the living area and the kitchen by means of a white enameled iron table. A study has been perfectly incorporated into the living area.

À l'exception des chambres à coucher, les pièces de cet appartement à étage unique sont interconnectées à la fois dans leur structure et dans leur aspect. La salle à manger devient ainsi le point de communication entre le séjour et la cuisine, grâce à une table de fer laqué blanc. Un bureau a été parfaitement intégré dans le séjour.

In questo appartamento distribuito su un solo piano tutte le stanze sono collegate tra loro, sia a livello strutturale che estetico, a eccezione della zona notte. La sala da pranzo, grazie a un leggero tavolino in ferro laccato bianco, è il punto di collegamento tra salotto e cucina. In salotto è stata creata una zona ufficio che si integra perfettamente con il resto della zona giorno.

In dieser einstöckigen Wohnung sind außer dem Schlafbereich alle Räume sowohl auf struktureller als auch auf ästhetischer Ebene miteinander verbunden. Der Essbereich bildet mithilfe eines leichten Tisches aus weiß lackiertem Eisen die Verbindung von Wohnzimmer und Küche. Im Wohnzimmer wurde ein Arbeitsplatz gestaltet, der sich perfekt in den Wohnbereich einfügt.

In dit appartement van een verdieping zijn alle vertrekken met elkaar verbonden, zowel op structureel als esthetisch niveau, behalve de slaapzone. De eethoek is d.m.v. een lichte wit gelakte ijzeren tafel de schakel tussen de zitkamer en de keuken. In de living is een werkruimte gecreëerd die perfect in de woonruimte past.

En este apartamento de una sola planta todas las estancias están interconectadas, tanto a nivel estructural como estético, excepto la zona de noche. El comedor, mediante una ligera mesa en hierro lacado blanco, es el nexo entre el salón y la cocina. En el salón se ha creado una zona de despacho que se integra a la perfección en el mismo.

Cartier

INGLES

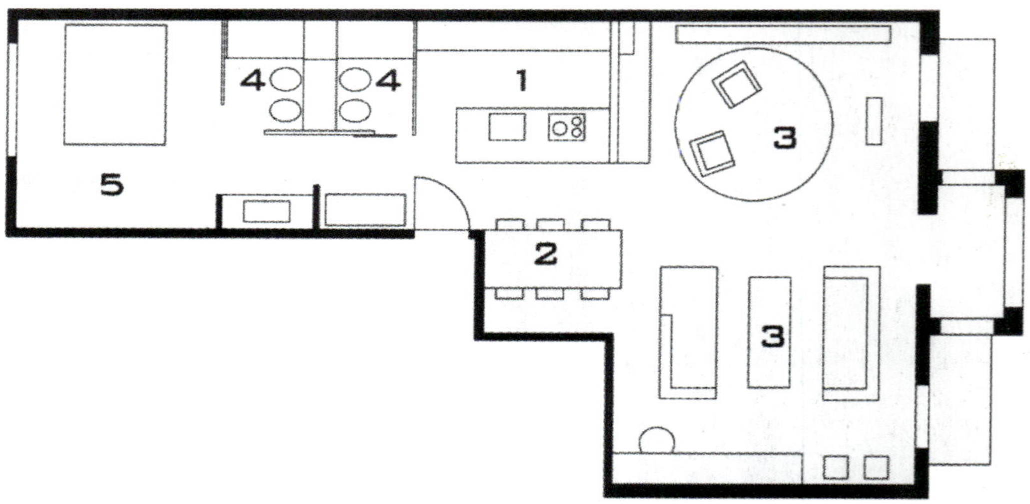

Floor plan / Grundriss / Plan
Plattegrond / Pianta / Planta

1. Kitchen / Küche / Cuisine / Keuken / Cucina / Cocina
2. Dining room / Eßzimmer / Salle à manger / Eetkamer / Stanza da pranzo / Comedor
3. Living room / Wohnzimmer / Séjour / Woonkamer / Stanz a di soggiorno / Sala de estar
4. Bathroom / Bad / Salle de bains / Badkamer / Bagno / Baño
5. Bedroom / Schlafzimmer / Chambre / Slaapkamer / Camera da letto / Dormitorio

APARTMENT IN **CABRILS**

Oriol Moya // www.440-bcn.com

This home combines a rational arrangement of furnishings with open, comfortable, and ordered spaces, laid out over three floors, with each covering an area of 70 m²/750 sq ft. The ample entrance hall offers an idea of the total size of the space, enhanced by the transparency of the stairs leading to the upper level where the bedrooms are located.

Cet intérieur combine un arrangement rationnel de l'ameublement avec des espaces ouverts confortables et ordonnés, répartis sur trois étages de 70 m² chacun. Le vaste hall d'entrée donne une idée des dimensions de l'espace total, mises en valeur par la transparence de l'escalier qui mène à l'étage supérieur où se trouvent les chambres.

Questa abitazione combina la distribuzione razionale degli arredi con spazi aperti, pratici e ordinati, suddivisi in tre piani di 70 m² ciascuno. L'ampio ingresso consente di apprezzare le dimensioni dello spazio totale tramite la trasparenza della scala di accesso al piano superiore, destinato alle camere da letto.

Diese Wohnung kombiniert auf drei Etagen mit jeweils 70 m² Fläche eine rationelle Anordnung der Möbel mit offenen, bequemen und geordneten Räumen. Die großzügige Diele erlaubt es, durch die Transparenz der Treppe, die zum oberen Stockwerk mit den Schlafzimmern führt, die Dimensionen des gesamten Raums zu würdigen.

Deze woning combineert een weloverwogen indeling van het meubilair met open, comfortabele en opgeruimde ruimtes, verdeeld over drie verdiepingen van elk 70 m². De ruime hal laat de dimensie van de totale ruimte via de transparantie van de trap naar de bovenverdieping, waar de slaapkamers zich bevinden, zien.

Esta vivienda combina la distribución racional del mobiliario con espacios abiertos, cómodos y ordenados, repartidos en tres plantas de 70 m² cada una. El amplio recibidor permite apreciar la dimensión total del apartamento a través de la escalera transparente que conduce a la planta superior, destinada a los dormitorios.

APARTMENT IN **FIGUERES**

Ruiz Narvaiza Associats // www.elenaruiz.com

This space is marked by the imposing presence of the staircase, which divides the home into different spaces. The living area features a fireplace, around which the seating system is arranged, leaving space for a separate reading area. The dining area follows, presided over by a huge lamp.

L'espace est marqué par la présence imposante de l'escalier, qui divise l'intérieur en différents espaces. Le séjour est doté d'une cheminée autour de laquelle sont installés les sièges, ce qui dégage un espace séparé pour la lecture. La salle à manger vient ensuite, dominée par une énorme lampe.

Questo spazio è caratterizzato dall'imponente presenza della scala che suddivide i vari ambienti della casa. Il salotto comprende un caminetto intorno al quale si articolano le sedute, con una zona indipendente dedicata alla lettura. Troviamo poi la sala da pranzo, dove domina una lampada a pavimento di grandi dimensioni.

Dieser Raum wird durch die beeindruckende Treppe geprägt, die die verschiedenen Innenräume der Wohnung abteilt. Das Wohnzimmer verfügt über einen Kamin, um den die Sitzgruppe angeordnet ist, und über eine separate Leseecke. Im Anschluss befindet sich der Essbereich, der von einer großformatigen Stehlampe beherrscht wird.

In deze ruimte neemt de trap, die de verschillende kamers van de woning verdeelt, een belangrijke rol in. De woonkamer heeft een open haard met daar omheen de zithoek met een afzonderlijke leeszone. In aansluiting op deze ruimte bevindt zich de eethoek met een zeer grote staande lamp.

El apartamento está marcado por la imponente presencia de la escalera, que divide la vivienda en diferentes espacios. El salón dispone de chimenea, a cuyo alrededor se articulan los asientos, con una zona de lectura indepenciente. A continuación, se encuentra el comedor, presidido por una lámpara de pie ce grandes dimensiones.

DALÍ
Barcelona arquitectura

APARTMENT **WHITE SPACE**

Hanrahan Meyers Architects // www.hanrahanmeyers.com

The design of this project aimed to create a flowing space that adapted to the needs of a couple who were devoted art collectors. Although the space is distinguished for its gentle use of a single color, the different textures, hues, and materials contribute to create a warm and welcoming ambience in a home that overlooks New York's Central Park West.

Le concept de ce projet visait à créer un espace fluide adapté aux exigences d'un couple de collectionneurs passionnés. L'espace ainsi réalisé se distingue par le sobre usage d'une couleur unique et par les différentes textures, nuances et matières qui contribuent à créer une ambiance accueillante et chaleureuse dans cet appartement qui domine l'ouest de Central Park, à New York.

L'obiettivo del progetto era quello di creare uno spazio fluido che si adattasse alle necessità di una coppia interessata a collezionare opere d'arte. Anche se lo spazio si distingue per un monocromatismo leggero, i diversi materiali, toni e forme contribuiscono a creare un ambiente accogliente e caldo, totalmente aperto verso Central Park West.

Das Ziel dieses Projekts bestand darin, weite Räume zu schaffen, die auf die Bedürfnissen eines Kunstsammler-Paares abgestimmt sind. Obwohl sich der Raum durch eine sanfte einheitliche Farbgebung auszeichnet, tragen die vorhandenen verschiedenen Texturen, Töne und Materialien dazu bei, eine warme und einladende Atmosphäre zu schaffen. Die Wohnung ist zum Central Park West hin vollkommen offen.

Het doel van het project is een vloeiende ruimte te creëren die zich aanpassen aan de behoeften van de eigenaars, een stel dat zich aan het verzamelen van kunstwerken wijdt. Hoewel de ruimte zich onderscheidt door een zachte eenkleurige uitstraling dragen diverse texturen, kleuren en materialen er aan bij om een gezellige omgeving te creëren met uitzicht op Central Park West.

El objetivo del proyecto era crear un espacio fluido y que se adaptara a las necesidades de una pareja dedicada al coleccionismo de piezas de arte. Aunque el espacio se distingue por un monocromatismo suave, las diversas texturas, tonos y materiales existentes contribuyen a crear un entorno cálido y acogedor, abierto completamente al Central Park West de Nueva York.

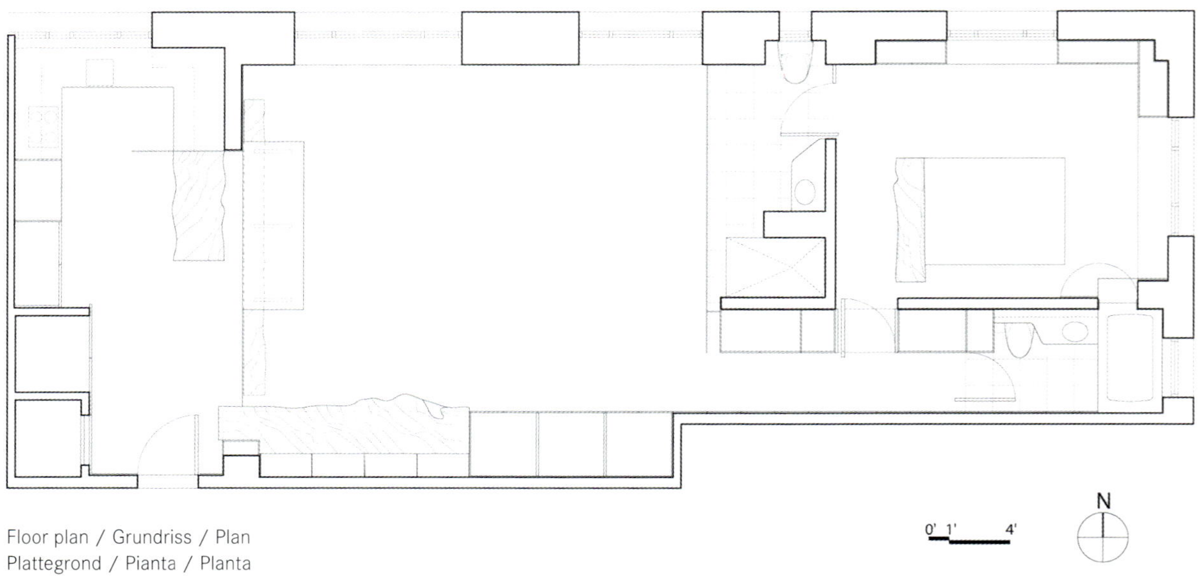

Floor plan / Grundriss / Plan
Plattegrond / Pianta / Planta

BERLIN ART NOW

APARTMENT **G.F.**

Raúl Campderrich / Air Projects // www.air-projects.com

This home features a large covered space on the terrace, enclosed by sliding aluminum shutters with adjustable louvers, a feature that creates interesting light effects on the interior while providing natural ventilation. The space that was gained from the terrace is designed with a social purpose and to offer its occupants a space for relaxation at any time of the year.

Cet intérieur offre un grand espace couvert en terrasse, fermé par des volets coulissants en aluminium à persiennes réglables. Cet élément crée d'intéressants effets de lumière à l'intérieur tout en assurant une ventilation naturelle. L'espace gagné grâce à la terrasse est destiné à la réception et sert de lieu de détente à tout moment de l'année pour les occupants.

Questa abitazione si caratterizza per un'ampia terrazza coperta con persiane scorrevoli composte da lastre di alluminio orientabili che creano un interessante gioco di luce all'interno, oltre a fornire una buona ventilazione naturale. Questo spazio interno, sottratto alla terrazza, è stato progettato al fine di disporre di una nuova zona sociale e relax in alcuni periodi dell'anno.

Diese Wohnung zeichnet sich durch einen großen überdachten Balkon mit Jalousien aus verstellbaren Aluminiumlamellen aus, die interessante Lichtspiele im Inneren und eine natürliche Belüftung ermöglichen. Dieser dem Balkon abgewonnene Raum wurde als neuer, zu jeder Jahreszeit benutzbarer Gemeinschafts- und Entspannungsbereich konzipiert.

Deze woning wordt gekenmerkt door een ruim overdekt terras met aluminium schuiflamellen, een hulpmiddel voor interessante lichteffecten in het interieur, alsmede voor natuurlijke ventilatie. Er is hier aan ruimte van het terras gewonnen. De bedoeling van deze ruimte was om het hele jaar over een nieuwe sociale en ontspanningszone te beschikken.

Esta vivienda se caracteriza por una amplia terraza cubierta con persianas correderas de lamas de aluminio orientables, recurso que aporta interesantes juegos de luz al interior, así como ventilación natural. Este espacio interior, ganado a la terraza, se diseñó con la intención de disponer de una nueva zona social y de relax durante cualquier época del año.

Nil

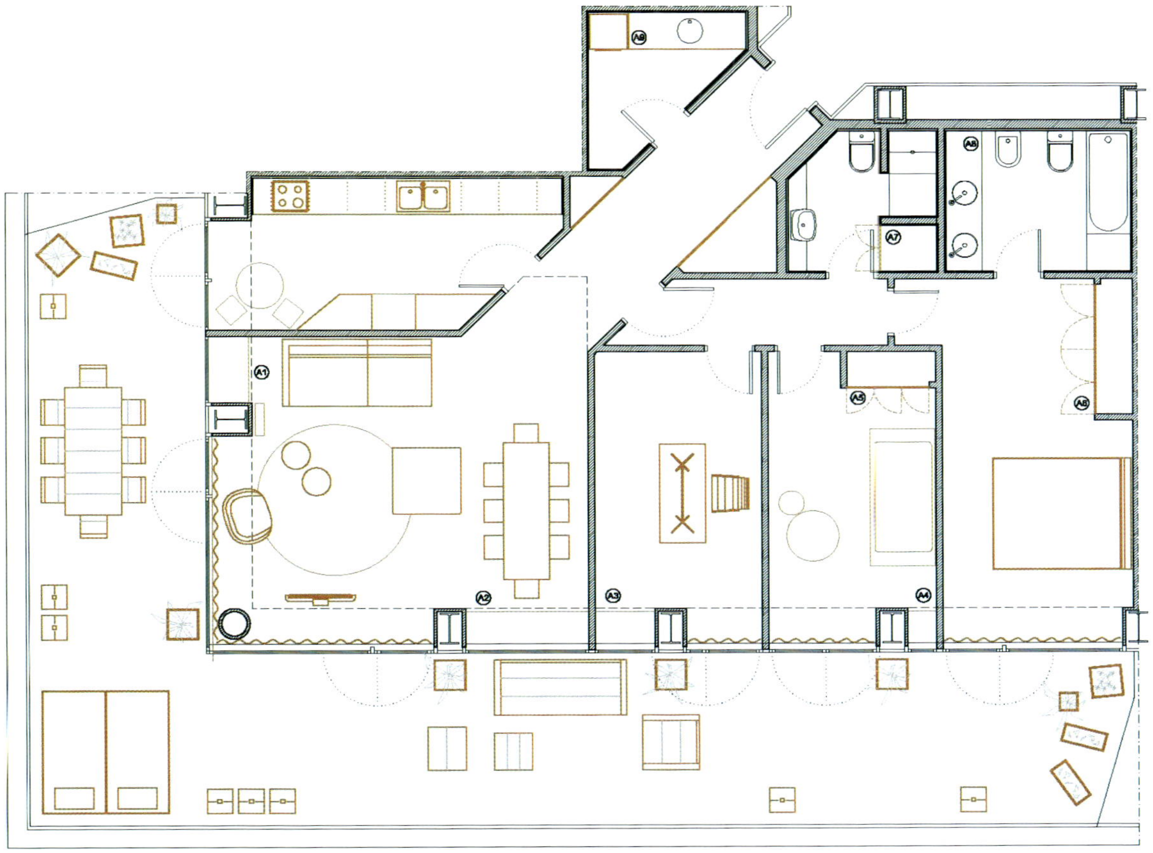

Floor plan / Grundriss / Plan
Plattegrond / Pianta / Planta

DUPLEX APARTMENT IN **SARRIÀ**

Eduard Samsó & Associats, C.B.

This apartment is laid out over two floors. A small entrance hall opens onto the kitchen, dining area and a slightly raised living room-library offering views of the garden. A stair twists up to the level containing three large bedrooms and two bathrooms.

Cet appartement se répartit sur deux étages. Une petite entrée ouvre sur la cuisine, la salle à manger et un séjour/bibliothèque légèrement surélevé offrant une vue sur le jardin. Un escalier en colimaçon conduit à l'étage où se trouvent trois grandes chambres et deux salles d'eau.

L'appartamento si sviluppa su due piani. Un piccolo distributore consente l'accesso alla cucina, alla sala da pranzo e a una sala-biblioteca che, essendo rialzata di alcuni centimentri, consente di vedere il giardino. Da qui parte una scala che porta alla zona notte con tre camere di grandi dimensioni e due bagni.

Diese Wohnung erstreckt sich über zwei Stockwerke. Eine kleine Diele führt in Küche, Esszimmer und das Wohnzimmer mit Bibliothek, das einige Zentimeter erhöht liegt und die Sicht in den Garten ermöglicht. Von dort aus führt eine Treppe in mehreren Windungen in den Ruhebereich mit drei großen Schlafzimmern und zwei Bädern.

Het appartement bestaat uit twee verdiepingen. Een kleine hal voert naar de keuken, de eethoek en een living met boekenkast die wat hoger ligt en uitzicht op de tuin heeft. Hier begint een trap met meerdere wentelingen die naar de slaapzone met drie grote slaapkamers en twee badkamers leidt.

El apartamento se desarrolla en dos plantas. Un pequeño distribuidor da paso a la cocina, al comedor y a un salón-biblioteca que, elevado unos centímetros, ofrece buenas vistas del jardín. Desde ahí parte una escalera que conduce a la zona de noche, con tres dormitorios de grandes dimensiones y dos baños.

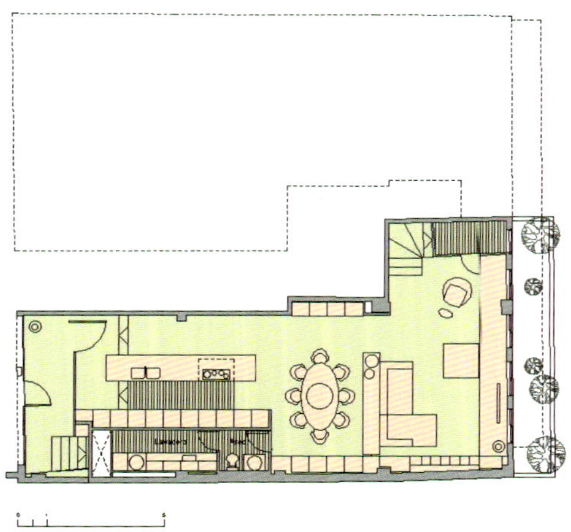

Ground floor / Erdgeschoss / Rez-de-chaussée
Begane grond / Piano terra/ Planta baja

Second floor / Zweites Obergeschoss / Second niveau
Tweede verdieping / Secondo piano / Segunda planta

PENTHOUSE IN A **DETACHED HOUSE**

GCA Arquitectes Associats // www.gcaarq.com

This attic is part of a single-family home with stunning views over the city of Barcelona and Collserola Park. This uppermost level contains the master bedroom and common areas, which are completely open to the exterior by means of a large terrace that serves as a large living area practically all year.

Ce grenier appartient à un appartement qui bénéficie de vues étonnantes sur Barcelone et sur le parc de Collserola. Ce niveau supérieur contient la chambre à coucher parentale ainsi que les parties communes, totalement ouvertes sur l'extérieur par une grande terrasse qui sert d'espace de séjour supplémentaire pratiquement toute l'année.

Questo attico fa parte di un'abitazione unifamiliare isolata che gode di una vista stupenda sulla città di Barcellona e sul parco di Collserola. Quest'ultimo livello è composto da una stanza principale e da zone comuni totalmente aperte verso l'esterno grazie a una grande terrazza che si converte in un ampio salotto, utilizzabile praticamente tutto l'anno.

Diese Dachwohnung ist Teil eines alleinstehenden Einfamilienhauses und bietet eine ausgezeichneter Sicht auf Barcelona und den Collserola-Park. Diese oberste Etage umfasst ein Hauptschlafzimmer und Gemeinschaftsbereiche, die dank einer großen Terrasse, welche praktisch das ganze Jahr über als riesiges Wohnzimmer dient, vollständig nach außen geöffnet sind.

Deze penthouse maakt deel uit van een vrijstaande eengezinswoning en heeft een voortreffelijk uitzicht op de Barcelona en het park Collserola. Deze bovenste verdieping is voorzien van een slaapkamer en gemeenschappelijke zones die dankzij een groot terras, dat praktisch het hele jaar als grote zitkamer kan worden gebruikt, naar de buitenwereld is gericht.

Este ático forma parte de una vivienda unifamiliar aislada, con unas excelentes vistas sobre la ciudad de Barcelona y el parque de Collserola. Este último nivel está dotado de habitación principal y zonas comunes, completamente abiertas al exterior gracias a una gran terraza que se convierte en un gran salón prácticamente todo el año.

PICASSO:
GUERRA I PAU

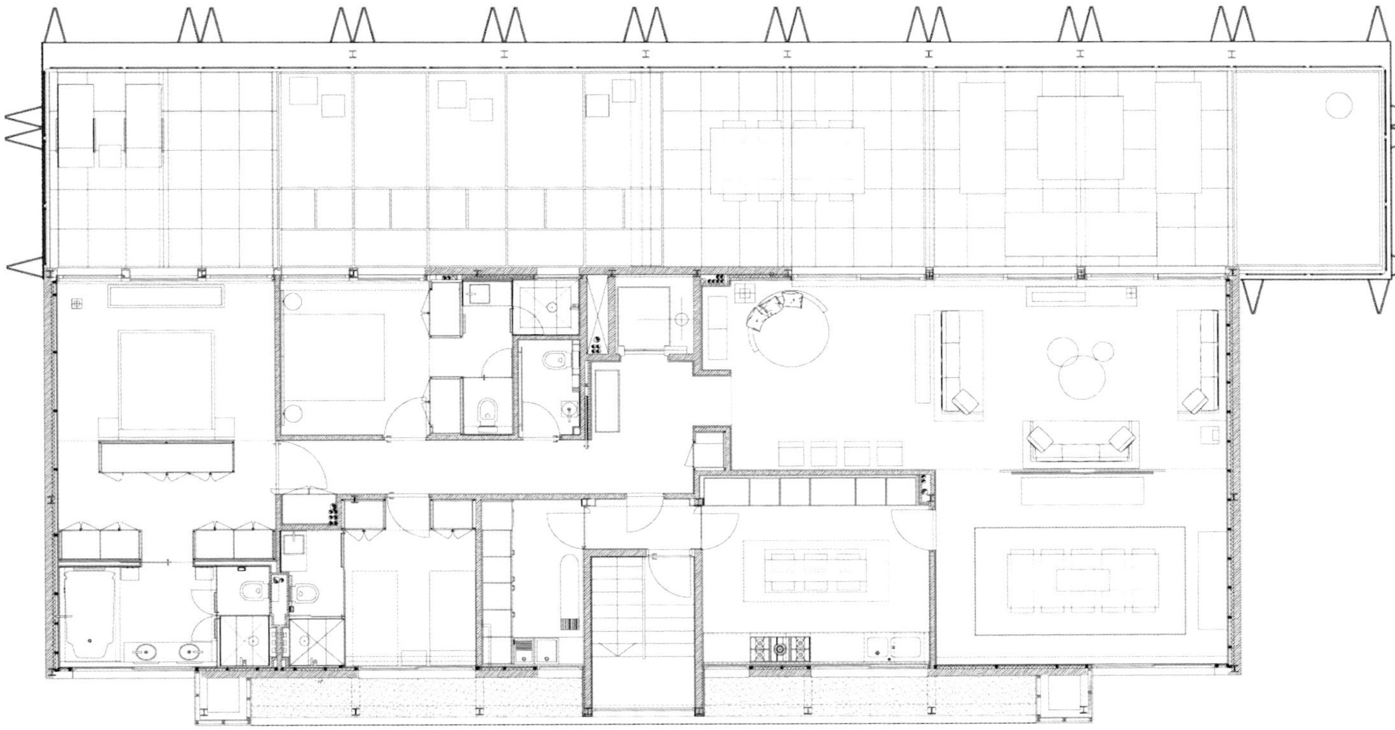

Floor plan / Grundriss / Plan
Plattegrond / Pianta / Planta

John Boyne
El niño con el pijama de rayas

APARTMENT **ZALABARDO**

Juli Barbastro
Interior Design: Ramón Zalabardo

This space is the combination of open areas that form a single block consisting of the entrance hall, living and dining areas, and the terrace. The layout makes total use of the daylight entering the home. One feature is the material used, such as wood and the Italian basaltina stone used to face a number of walls.

Cet espace d'habitation résulte de la combinaison d'espaces ouverts formant un bloc unique comprenant l'entrée, le séjour et la salle à manger, et la terrasse. La répartition exploite au maximum la lumière naturelle qui baigne l'appartement. Une des caractéristiques essentielles est l'emploi de matériaux comme le bois et le basaltina d'Italie, en placages muraux.

Questo spazio è il risultato della combinazione di spazi aperti che formano un unico blocco composto da ingresso, salotto, sala da pranzo e terrazza, tutti disposti per sfruttare al massimo la luce naturale. Si noti la scelta dei materiali come il legno e la pietra basaltina italiana che riveste alcune pareti.

Dieser Raum ist das Ergebnis der Kombination von offenen Bereichen, die einen einzigen Block bilden, der aus Empfangsbereich, Wohnzimmer, Esszimmer und Terrasse besteht und zur vollständigen Ausnutzung des einfallenden Tageslichts konzipiert wurde. Die verwendeten Materialien wie Holz und italienischer Basaltstein, mit dem einige Wände verkleidet sind, stechen besonders hervor.

Deze woning is het resultaat van de combinatie van open ruimtes die één enkel blok vormen, bestaand uit de hal, zit- en eethoek en terras, allemaal zodanig opgesteld dat het natuurlijke licht optimaal benut kan worden. Opvallend zijn de gekozen materialen, zoals hout en Italiaans lavasteen waarmee een aantal wanden is bekleed.

Este espacio es el resultado de la combinación de espacios abiertos que forman un único bloque, compuesto por recibidor, salón, comedor y terraza, todos ellos dispuestos para un total aprovechamiento de la luz natural. Destaca la selección de materiales empleados, como la madera y la piedra basaltina italiana de algunas de las paredes.

CHOCOLAT FACTORY

CHOCOLAT FACTORY

DavidBailey CHASING RAINBOWS

212

APARTMENT **VARINIA**

Inés Rodríguez, Raúl Campderrich / Air Projects // www.air-projects.com

This apartment naturally identifies with its occupants: a young couple seeking a comfortable and functional home with a casual style. The apartment is divided into two very separate areas: a large open-plan space containing the living and dining areas and the kitchen, separated by a sliding door, and the sleeping quarters.

Cet appartement s'identifie naturellement à ses occupants : un jeune couple recherchant un intérieur à la fois confortable et fonctionnel, dans un style décontracté. L'intérieur est donc divisé en deux zones distinctes : un grand espace en plan ouvert pour le séjour, la salle à manger et la cuisine (séparée par une porte coulissante), et les quartiers privés.

Questo appartamento si identifica naturalmente con chi lo abita: una coppia giovane che cerca comodità e funzionalità, con un'estetica informale. L'abitazione è divisa in due zone ben differenziate: uno spazio aperto e ampio che ospita sala da pranzo, salotto e cucina, separati da una porta scorrevole, e la zona notte.

Dieses Apartment passt auf natürliche Weise zu seinen Bewohnern, einem jungen Paar, das eine bequeme und funktionale, unkonventionell gestaltete Wohnung suchte. Die Wohnung ist in zwei deutlich abgegrenzte Bereiche aufgeteilt: in einen hellen, großen Raum, der den Essbereich, das Wohnzimmer und die durch eine Schiebetür abgeteilte Küche umfasst, und einen Raum für den Schlafbereich.

Dit appartement wordt op natuurlijke wijze met de bewoners ervan geïdentificeerd: een jong stel dat een comfortabele en functionele woonruimte met een informele uitstraling wil. De woning is verdeeld in twee duidelijk van elkaar te onderscheiden zones: een lichte, grote ruimte waar zich de eethoek, living en keuken bevinden die door een schuifdeur zijn gescheiden van de slaapzone.

Este apartamento se identifica de forma natural con sus ocupantes: una pareja joven que busca un entorno cómodo y funcional de estética informal. La vivienda se divide en dos zonas bien diferenciacas: un espacio diáfano y amplio que alberga el comedor, la sala de estar y la cocina, separados por una puerta corredera, y la zona de noche.

A British Film Institute Release
accenture
AUDREY HEPBURN
GEORGE PEPPARD
"Looks better than ever the definitive Hepburn movie"
"Eternally chic"
"A must for every fashionista"
Breakfast at Tiffany's
NEAL EBSEN BALSAM MICKEY ROONEY

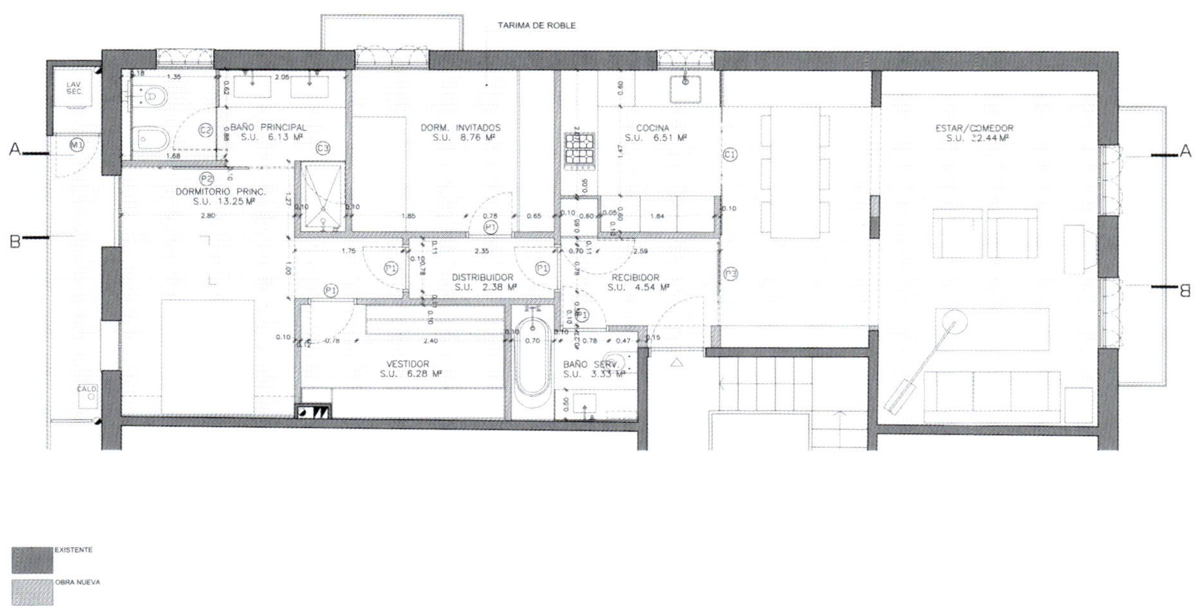

Floor plan / Grundriss / Plan
Plattegrond / Pianta / Planta

SMALL FAMILY HOUSE **OVERLOOKING BARCELONA**

GCA Arquitectes Associats // www.gcaarq.com

Design for a home set away from the street but open to the exterior, where views and exposure to daylight coincide. Natural materials feature throughout the interior: oak floors, natural gray stone in bathrooms, stainless steel in the kitchen, and white paint and stucco finishes on walls, enhancing the lighting.

Projet pour un appartement à l'écart de la rue, mais ouvert sur l'extérieur, où la vue coïncide avec la prise de lumière. L'intérieur entier est fait de matériaux naturels : parquets en chêne, pierre grise naturelle dans les salles de bains, acier inoxydable dans la cuisine, peinture et finitions de stuc blanches sur les murs, pour augmenter la luminosité.

Proposta di un'abitazione isolata dalla strada, ma con una chiara esposizione verso l'esterno, dove coincidono panorama e orientamento solare. All'interno, i materiali sono naturali: rovere nei pavimenti, pietra naturale grigia nei bagni, acciaio in cucina, pittura e stucchi bianchi alle pareti per trasmettere maggiore luminosità.

Beispiel für die Gestaltung einer von der Straße abgewandten Wohnung, die dank ihrer großen Südfenster jedoch viel Tageslicht einfallen lässt und eine unverbaute Aussicht bietet. Im Inneren wurden Naturmaterialien verwendet: Eiche für den Bodenbelag, kieselgrauer Naturstein in den Bädern, Stahl in der Küche und weiß gestrichener Putz an den Wänden, der die Helligkeit dieses Zuhauses unterstreicht.

Een vrijstaande woning, afgezonderd van de straat, maar die duidelijk met buiten is verbonden en waar het uitzicht en de ligging op de zon overeenkomen. Binnenshuis zijn natuurlijke materialen gebruikt: eikenhouten vloeren, grijze natuursteen in de badkamers, staal in de keuken, en wit geschilderde en gepleisterde wanden, waardoor de verlichting wordt geaccentueerd.

Se trata de una propuesta de una vivienda aislada de la calle, pero abierta al exterior, que ofrece buenas vistas y orientación al sol. En el interior, los materiales son naturales: roble en los pavimentos, piedra natural grisácea en los baños, acero en la cocina, y pintados y estucos blancos en la paredes, realzándose así la iluminación.

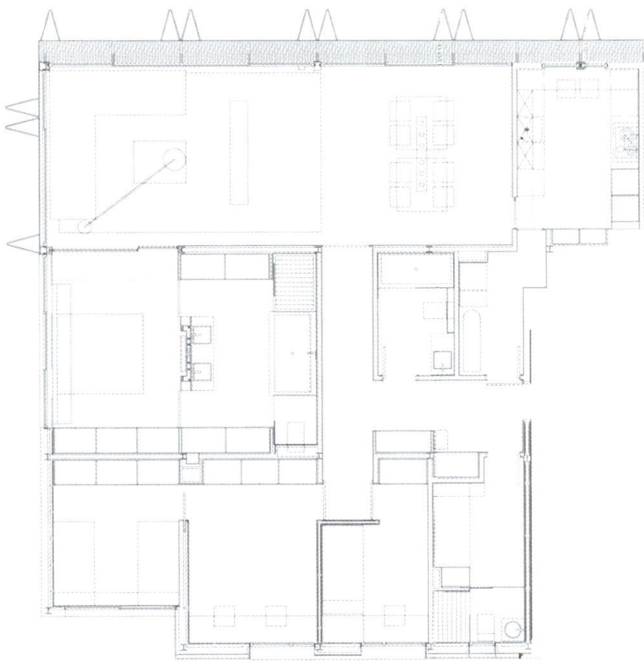

Floor plan / Grundriss / Plan
Plattegrond / Pianta / Planta

CASAS

BLINK.
CASAS
ARCHITECTURE NOW!
HABANOS
Arquitectura internacional

EMPORDÀ
MICHAEL CRICHTON
NOAH GORDON
BENVINGUT AL MON REAL
INTELIGENCIA EMOCIONAL
Daniel Goleman
FURIA
EL ÚLTIMO JUDÍO
NOAH GORDON
THOMAS HARRIS
LOS ASESINATOS DE MANHATTAN
MATILDE ASENSI EL ÚLTIMO CATÓN
ISABEL ALLENDE
DANIEL MASON EL AFINADOR DE PIANOS
Eduardo Mendoza
INDIA UNA CIVILIZACIÓN HERIDA

arquitectura

GEIS LOFT

Slade Architecture // www.sladearch.com

This home is the result of environmental criteria applied to the refurbishment of a duplex apartment. In order to make maximum use of the available space, the lower treads of the staircase leading to the upper level are part of the kitchen cabinets.

Die Renovierung eines zweigeschossigen Gebäudes unter ökologischen Aspekten führte zu dieser Wohnung. Um den verfügbaren Raum maximal auszunutzen, bilden die Stufen, die zur oberen Etage führen, einen Teil der Küchenschränke.

Cette résidence résulte de l'application des critères écologiques à la rénovation d'un appartement en duplex. Afin d'exploiter au maximum l'espace disponible, les marches inférieures de l'escalier menant à l'étage sont intégrées aux rayonnages de rangement de la cu sine.

Deze woning is het resultaat van de verbouwing van een duplex met milieuvriendelijke criteria. Teneinde de beschikbare ruimte maximaal te benutten, maken de eerste traptreden naar de bovenverdieping deel uit van de keukenkasten.

La ristrutturazione di un'abitazione su due piani applicando criteri ecologici ha dato vita a questo progetto. Al fine di sfruttare al massimo lo spazio disponibile, i primi gradini di accesso al piano superiore sono stati utilizzati come elementi contenitivi per la cucina.

Esta vivienda es el resultado de la renovación de un dúplex con criterios ecológicos. Con el objetivo de aprovechar al máximo el espacio disponible, los primeros peldaños de acceso a la planta superior forman parte de los armarios de la cocina.

Earthsong

Earthsong

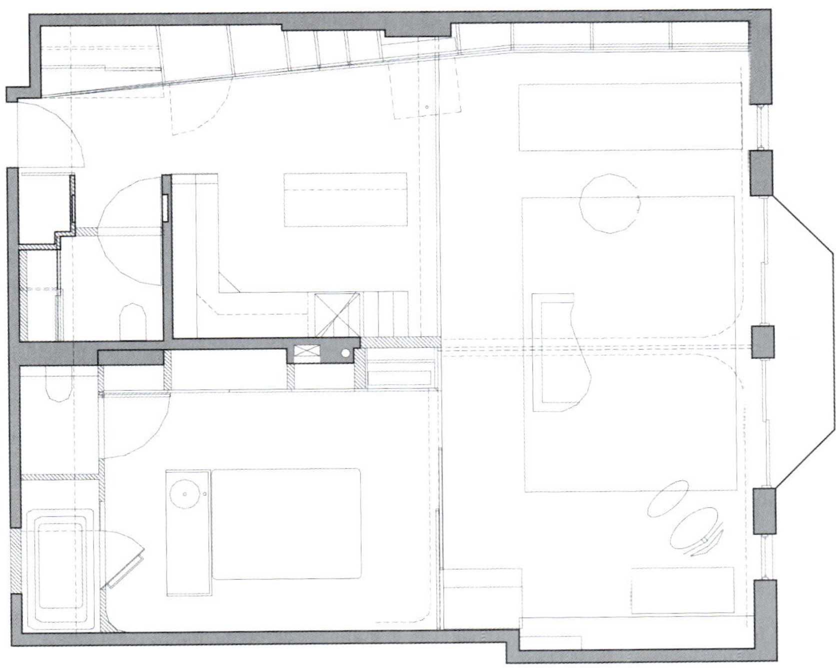

Floor plan / Grundriss / Plan
Plattegrond / Pianta / Planta

Rody

PENTHOUSE IN **SALOU**

Mamen Domingo and Ernest Ferré // www.domingoferre.com
Interior Design: Maite Aymení

The design of this seafront apartment involved a radical transformation. It involved opening the home out to the exterior, turning it into a glass box facing the sea. A large open area was achieved by reducing the sleeping areas and adding the space gained to the living and dining areas and the kitchen.

La conception de cet appartement du front de mer impliquait une transformation radicale. Il fallait ouvrir la demeure sur l'extérieur, en la métamorphosant en une boîte de verre face à la mer. On a donc obtenu une grande surface ouverte en réduisant les chambres à coucher et en ajoutant l'espace gagné au séjour, à la salle à manger et à la cuisine.

Per questo appartamento, ubicato di fronte al mare, è stata proposta una trasformazione radicale. L'intervento consiste nell'aprire completamente l'abitazione all'esterno per convertirla in una scatola di vetro rivolta verso il mare. Si è riusciti a ottenere uno spazio ampio limitando al massimo la superficie della zona notte e integrando quello della zona giorno, della cucina e della sala da pranzo.

Für dieses am Meer gelegene Apartment wurde ein radikaler Umbau vorgeschlagen. Die gesamte Wohnung sollte nach außen hin geöffnet und in einen Glaskasten mit Meerblick verwandelt werden. Das Ergebnis der strengen Begrenzung der Fläche für den Schlafbereich ist ein großzügiges Zuhause mit kombiniertem Wohnzimmer, Küche und Essbereich.

Voor dit aan zee liggende appartament is een radicale verbouwing voorgesteld. Hierbij werd de woning volledig naar buiten toe geopend en veranderd in een glazen box met zeezicht. Het is gelukt om een grote ruimte te creëren waarbij het slaapgedeelte zo veel mogelijk is beperkt en de living, keuken en eethoek een ruimte innemen.

Para este apartamento, situado frente al mar, se ha propuesto una transformación radical. La intervención consiste en abrir completamente la vivienda al exterior, convirtiéndola en una caja de cristal que mira hacia el agua. Se ha logrado obtener un espacio amplio limitando al máximo la superficie de la zona de noche e integrando en una misma área el salón, la cocina y el comedor.

HENRY MOORE
Joan Miró

HENRY MOORE
Joan Miró

MARK TOBEY
THE IMPRESSIONISTS

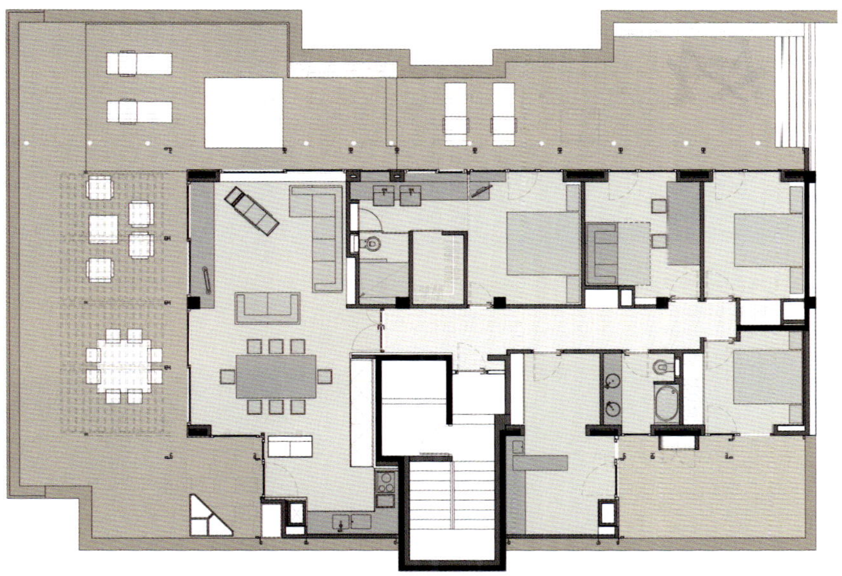

Floor plan / Grundriss / Plan
Plattegrond / Pianta / Planta

APARTMENT **BERTRAN**

Alonso Balaguer y Arquitectos Asociados // www.alonsobalaguer.com
Interior Design: Àmbit Interiors

Located in a hillside district of Barcelona, this home was designed with the aim of removing all possible visual barriers, creating a singular, fluid space where all the different areas are brought together through the set of exposed concrete load-bearing walls.

Situé sur les hauteurs de Barcelone, cet intérieur a été conçu dans le but de supprimer tous les obstacles possibles à la vue. Cela crée un espace unique et fluide où toutes les aires différentes sont mises en rapport par le jeu des murs porteurs en béton brut.

Questa casa, situata nella zona alta di Barcellona, è stata realizzata con l'obiettivo di eliminare tutte le barriere visive possibili creando un ambiente unico e fluido che colleghi le varie zone e che abbia come filo conduttore l'insieme delle pareti strutturali in cemento a vista che configura i muri portanti.

Diese Wohnung, die sich im höher gelegenen Teil Barcelonas befindet, wurde mit dem Ziel entworfen, möglichst alle visuellen Barrieren zu vermeiden und ein einzigartiges, fließendes Ambiente zu schaffen, das die verschiedenen Bereiche miteinander verbindet. Als roter Faden dienen die Strukturmauern aus Sichtbeton, aus denen die tragenden Wände bestehen.

Deze woning in een hooggelegen wijk van Barcelona is ontworpen met als doel alle mogelijke visuele barrières op te heffen en een unieke en vloeiende ruimte te creëren waar de verschillende zones elkaar opvolgen, en waarvan de structurele muren van zichtbaar beton die de dragende muren vormen de leidraad zijn.

Esta residencia, situada en la zona alta de Barcelona, se ha desarrollado con el objetivo de eliminar todas las barreras visuales posibles, creando un ambiente único y fluido que vincula las distintas zonas, y que tiene como hilo conductor el conjunto de muros estructurales de hormigón visto que configura las paredes maestras.

HELMU
HELMUT LANG
est.986
FINEST CLOTHING AND LUXURY GOODS FOR MEN AND WOMEN
HELMUT
HELMUT LANG

Enjoy!
Coca-Cola

Enjoy!

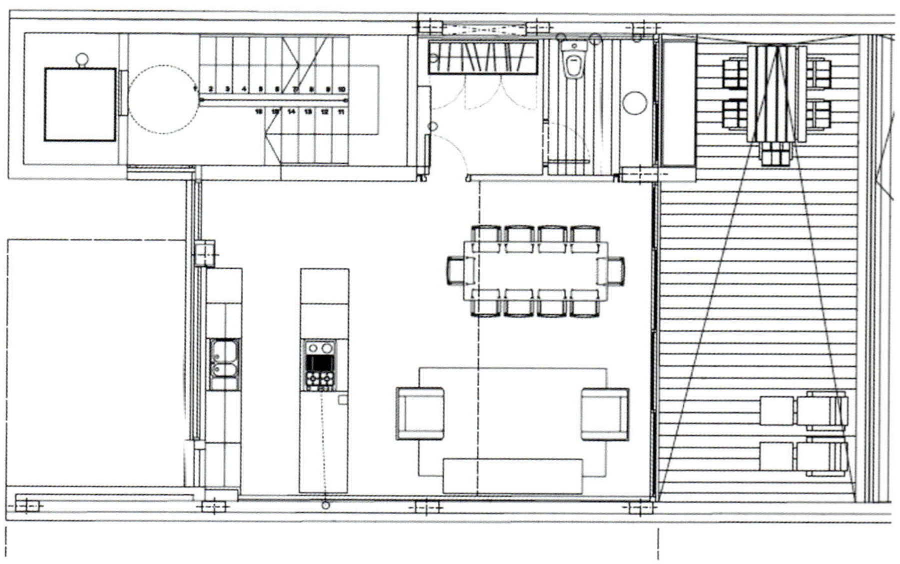

Floor plan / Grundriss / Plan
Plattegrond / Pianta / Planta

PARISIAN

BAUHAUS

COTE
DE LA

APARTMENT IN **VALLVIDRERA**

Victoria Giró
Interior Design: Adela Cabré

Wood is made into a dominant feature of this home: iroko wood was used on walls, the staircase, and the kitchen and bathroom cabinets, while sucupira hardwood was used on the dining area floor and in much of the furniture, most of which was designed by interior designer Adela Cabré.

Le bois est une caractéristique dominante de cet intérieur : on a utilisé du bois d'iroko pour les murs, l'escalier, le mobilier de la cuisine et de la salle d'eau ; du bois de sucupira, en revanche, pour le sol de la salle à manger et pour une bonne partie du mobilier conçu pour l'essentiel par Adela Cabré, styliste d'intérieur.

Il legno acquisisce un ruolo di protagonista in questa abitazione: iroko su pareti, scala e mobili di cucina e bagno e sucupira sul pavimento della sala da pranzo oltre che in gran parte degli arredi, molti dei quali sono progettati dalla designer di interni Adela Cabré.

Holz spielt eine bedeutende Rolle in dieser Wohnung: Iroko an den Wänden, auf der Treppe und für die Küchen- und Badezimmermöbel und Sucupira als Bodenbelag des Esszimmers und für einen großen Teil der Möbel, die in der Mehrzahl von der Innenarchitektin Adela Cabré entworfen wurden.

Het hout speelt een aanzienlijke rol in deze woning: iroko op de wanden, de trap en de keuken- en badkamermeubels en sucupira op de vloer van de woonkamer, net als veel van de meubels, de meeste ontworpen door de binnenhuisarchitecte Adela Cabré.

La madera adquiere un notable protagonismo en esta vivienda: iroko en las paredes, la escalera y los muebles de la cocina y el baño, y sucupira en el pavimento del comedor y en gran parte del mobiliario, la mayoría diseñado por la interiorista Adela Cabré.

APARTMENT IN **MADRID**

Rocío Fueyo

The high ceilings of this small Madrid apartment made it possible to create a mezzanine space for the bedrooms, with the living area, kitchen, bathroom, and walk-in closet on the lower level. The original beams and columns were retained and eight small windows were opened in the side walls to allow daylight to enter.

Les plafonds élevés de ce petit appartement madrilène ont permis de créer en mezzanine un espace pour les chambres à coucher, tandis que le séjour, la cuisine, la salle d'eau et le *dressing* sont en bas. On a gardé les poutres et les colonnes d'origine, et l'on a percé huit petites fenêtres dans les murs latéraux pour permettre la pénétration de la lumière du jour.

I soffitti alti di questo piccolo appartamento di Madrid hanno consentito di creare una doppia altezza, distribuendo le camere nella zona superiore e salotto, cucina, bagno e guardaroba nella zona inferiore. Sono state lasciate le travi e le colonne originali della casa e sono state aperte otto piccole finestre sulle pareti mediane per consentire l'ingresso di luce naturale.

Die hohen Decken dieses kleinen Apartments in Madrid erlaubten die Einrichtung einer Zwischenebene, wobei die Schlafzimmer den oberen und Wohnzimmer, Küche, Bad und Ankleidebereich den unteren Bereich einnehmen. Die Balken und Originalsäulen des Hauses sind erhalten geblieben und es wurden acht kleine Fenster in die Zwischenwände eingebaut, um natürliches Licht einzulassen.

Dankzij de hoge plafonds van dit kleine appartement in Madrid is het mogelijk om een tussenverdieping te creëren. Op de bovenste bevinden zich de slaapkamers en beneden de salon, keuken, badkamer en garderobe. De oorspronkelijke balken en zuilen van het huis zijn bewaard gebleven en er zijn acht kleine ramen in de tussenmuren gemaakt die voor natuurlijke verlichting zorgen.

Los techos elevados de este pequeño apartamento en Madrid han permitido crear una doble altura, y distribuir los dormitorios en la zona superior, y el salón, la cocina, el baño y el vestidor en la inferior. Se han mantenido las vigas y las columnas originales de la casa y se han abierto ocho pequeñas ventanas en los muros medianeros para que proporcionen iluminación natural.

ROLLO

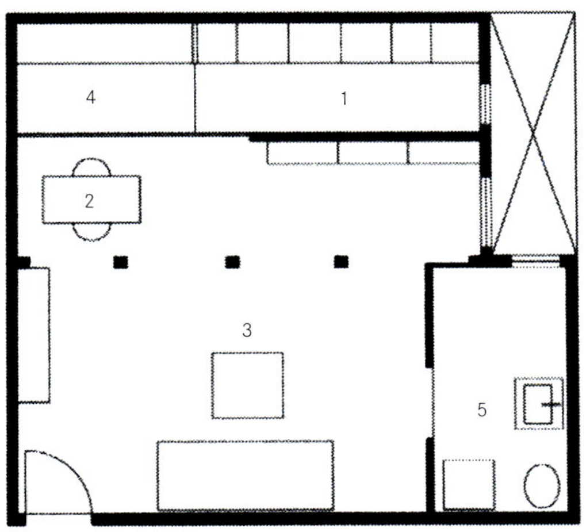

Ground floor / Erdgeschoss / Rez-de-chaussée
Begane grond / Piano terra/ Planta baja

1. Kitchen / Küche / Cuisine
   Keuken / Cucina / Cocina
2. Dining room / Eßzimmer / Salle à manger
   Eetkamer / Stanza da pranzo / Comedor
3. Living room / Wohnzimmer / Séjour
   Woonkamer / Stanza di soggiorno / Sala de estar
4. Bathroom / Bad / Salle de bains
   Badkamer / Bagno / Baño
5. Bedroom / Schlafzimmer / Chambre
   Slaapkamer / Camera da letto / Dormitorio

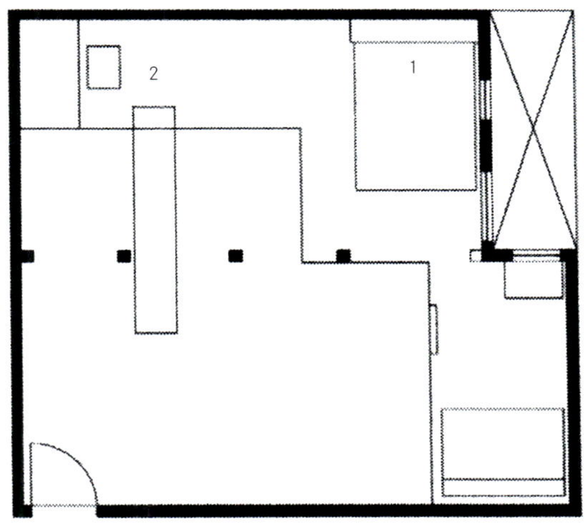

Second floor / Zweites Obergeschoss / Second niveau
Tweede verdieping / Secondo piano / Segunda planta

1. Bedroom / Schlafzimmer / Chambre
   Slaapkamer / Camera da letto / Dormitorio
2. Study / Arbeitszimmer / Bureau
   Studio / Studio / Estudio

APARTMENT **VAN DOREN**

James Slade / Slade Architecture // www.sladearch.com

This small apartment serves two purposes; it is both a home and a place for work and gatherings. The program is laid out over two levels, the lower one housing the common areas and upper level containing the bedroom, walk-in closet, office, bathroom, and a small living area.

Ce petit appartement a une triple destination : il est à la fois lieu d'habitation, lieu de travail et lieu de réception. Le programme se répartit sur deux niveaux, celui du bas accueillant les zones communes, celui du haut étant réservé à la chambre à coucher, au *dressing*, au bureau, à la salle d'eau et à un petit séjour.

Questo appartamento di dimensioni ridotte svolge una doppia funzione: abitazione e spazio di lavoro e di riunione. La struttura è organizzata su due piani: al livello inferiore troviamo la zona giorno mentre al livello superiore sono stati inseriti camera, guardaroba, ufficio, bagno e un piccolo salotto.

Dieses kleine Apartment erfüllt eine doppelte Funktion: es ist Wohnung und gleichzeitig Arbeitsplatz und Treffpunkt. In der unteren der zwei Etagen befindet sich der Tagesbereich, das obere Stockwerk beherbergt die Schlafzimmer, einen Ankleideraum, Büro, Bad und einen kleinen Wohnbereich.

Dit kleine appartement heeft een dubbele functie: woning en werk- en vergaderruimte. Het is verdeeld over twee niveaus met op de benedenverdieping het daggedeelte en op de bovenverdieping de slaapkamer, inloopkast, werkruimte en een kleine zithoek.

Este apartamento de reducidas dimensiones cumple una doble función: vivienda y espacio de trabajo y reunión. Así, el programa se resuelve en dos plantas en cuyo nivel inferior se ubicó la zona de día y en el superior se distribuyeron el dormitorio, el vestidor, la oficina, el baño y una pequeña zona de estar.

APARTMENT IN **EIVISSA**

Francisco Mangado // www.fmangado.com

This residential project aimed to break with the stereotyped décor connected with island of Ibiza. The home adapts to the uneven terrain to create a series of intertwines volumes and a succession of vertical planes with great expressive intensity. White is naturally the leading feature.

Ce programme résidentiel visait à casser les stéréotypes de décoration liés à l'île d'Ibiza. La demeure s'adapte ainsi aux inégalités de terrain pour créer une série de volumes imbriqués et une succession de plans verticaux dotés d'une grande intensité expressive. Le blanc reste naturellement la caractéristique principale.

Questo progetto residenziale tenta di rompere con i convenzionalismi decorativi tipici dell'isola di Ibiza. L'abitazione si adatta alla tortuosa orografia del terreno creando una serie di volumi che si mescolano tra loro dando vita a una successione di piani verticali di grande intensità espressiva. Ovviamente il colore bianco è il protagonista.

Dieses Wohnprojekt will mit dem Gestaltungs-Konventionalismus von Ibiza brechen. Die Wohnung passt sich der bergigen Struktur des Geländes an, indem eine Reihe von Räumen geschaffen wurde, die sich vermischen und eine Folge von senkrechten Flächen mit großer Ausdruckskraft schaffen. Natürlich spielt die Farbe Weiß die absolute Hauptrolle.

Dit woningproject wil met de decoratieve opvattingen van het eiland Ibiza breken. De woning past zich aan de kronkelige vormen van het terrein aan door de creatie van ruimtes die zich vermengen en een opeenvolging van verticale vlakken met een krachtige uitstraling vormen. Uiteraard speelt de kleur wit een absolute hoofdrol.

Este proyecto residencial busca romper con los estereotipos de la decoración de la isla ibicenca. La vivienda se adapta a la tortuosa orografía del terreno, creando una serie de volúmenes que se entremezclan y forman una sucesión de planos verticales de gran intensidad expresiva. Por supuesto, el color blanco es protagonista absoluto.

YOU MEET THE NICEST PEOPLE ON A HONDA
Nikon
SEIKO

APARTMENT **CALA MILLOR**

Vicenç Mulet / VMA Projectes // www.vma.cat

A bookcase that serves as both partition and storage unit is the feature of this common area, the furniture of which was also designed by the architect. The living area opens to the exterior and is flooded with daylight.

Ein Bücherregal, das gleichzeitig als Raumteiler dient, dominiert diesen Gemeinschaftsbereich, dessen Mobiliar vom Architekten selbst entworfen wurde. Das Wohnzimmer öffnet sich nach außen und ist in natürliches Licht getaucht.

Une bibliothèque servant à la fois de cloison et d'unité de rangement est la caractéristique de cet espace unifié dont l'ameublement a également été conçu par l'architecte. Le séjour est ouvert sur l'extérieur et baigne dans la lumière.

Een boekenkast die eveneens als tussenwand en opbergruimte fungeert heeft de overhand in deze gemeenschappelijke ruimte met meubilair dat door de architect zelf is ontworpen. De zitkamer komt uit op buiten en wordt overgoten met zonlicht.

Una libreria che funge da separatore spaziale e da elemento contenitivo presiede questa zona comune, con arredi progettati dallo stesso architetto. Il salotto si apre verso l'esterno ed è inondato di luce naturale.

Una librería que funciona tanto como elemento separador y como unidad de almacenaje preside esta zona común, con mobiliario diseñado por el propio arquitecto. El salón se abre al exterior y se inunda de luz natural.

CASAS
del Mundo

APARTMENT **ICARIA**

Meritxell Ribé / **Estudi Meritxell Ribé** // www.meritxellribe.com

This apartment covers 750 sq ft and features a living-dining area and kitchen occupying a single space. The sofa is used as an element that separates the spaces. Its color matches that of the kitchen furniture and the facing wall, bringing all the elements of this residential space into complete and homogenous integration.

Cet appartement couvre 70 m² et combine en un seul espace séjour, salle à manger et cuisine. Le canapé est utilisé comme élément de séparation des espaces. Sa couleur correspond à celle du mobilier de cuisine et du mur qui lui fait face, en intégrant de façon homogène et complète tous les éléments de cet espace résidentiel.

Questo appartamento di circa 70 m² integra in un solo spazio salotto, cucina e sala da pranzo. Nel salotto il divano funge da delimitatore spaziale. Cromaticamente si armonizza con gli arredi della cucina e la parete frontale consentendo un'integrazione completa e omogenea di tutti gli elementi di questo contesto residenziale.

In diesem ca 70 m² großen Apartment wurden Wohnzimmer, Küche und Essbereich in einen einzigen Raum integriert. Im Wohnzimmer fungiert das Sofa als Raumbegrenzung. Die Küchenmöbel harmonieren farblich mit der Stirnwand und ermöglichen somit die vollständige und einheitliche Einbettung aller Elemente in diesen Wohnbereich.

Dit appartement, van ongeveer 70 m², heeft in één ruimte een living, keuken en eethoek. In de zitkamer fungeert de bank als scheidingselement van de ruimte. Qua kleuren harmoniseert het keukenmeubi air en de voorwand, waardoor alle elementen van deze woonomgeving volledig en homogeen met elkaar integreren.

Este apartamento de unos 70 m² integra en un solo espacio salón, cocina y comedor. En el salón, el sofá actúa como elemento delimitador del espacio. Cromáticamente, armoniza con el mobiliario de la cocina y la pared frontal, lo que permite la integración completa y homogénea de todos los elementos de este entorno residencial.

silence of knowing, the certainty
the joy of giving, the smile for no
that is yielding, the look that
the sleep that is weightless, the
the trust of fate, the patience of time
of space, the certainty of right... gill
silence of knowing, the certainty of
the joy of giving, the smile for no reason,
that is yielding, the look that speaks
sleep that is weightless, the

APARTAMENT **N.A.**

Francisco Mangado // www.fmangado.com

Several design solutions are incorporated into this single space that combines a lounge area (marked by the contrast between black and white silk cushions), a study with a vertical bookstand, a living area with a marble fireplace, and a reading nook. The library features perforated metal columns and antiques.

Plusieurs solutions de stylisme sont incorporées dans cet espace unique combinant un salon (marqué par le contraste des coussins de soie blancs et noirs), un bureau doté d'une bibliothèque, un séjour avec cheminée et un coin lecture. La bibliothèque combine des colonnes en métal perforé et des objets anciens.

Spazio che integra varie soluzioni in un solo ambiente, unendo salotto (definito dal contrasto tra i cuscini di seta bianchi e neri), studio con scaffalatura verticale, zona giorno con caminetto rifinito in marmo e angolo lettura. Si impone la biblioteca, caratterizzata da colonne composite e pezzi provenienti da vari antiquari.

In diesem Zuhause wurden verschiedene Lösungen in ein einziges Zimmer integriert: das durch den Kontrast der weißen und schwarzen Seidenkissen geprägte Wohnzimmer, das Arbeitszimmer mit vertikalem Regal und der Aufenthaltsbereich mit Kamin mit Marmoreinfassung und Leseecke wurden vereint. Auffallend ist die Bibliothek mit Säulen aus Metall und Stücken, die aus verschiedenen Antiquariaten stammen.

Ruimte met diverse oplossingen in één vertrek: salon (die wordt gekenmerkt door het contrast tussen de witte en zwarte zijden kussens), studio met verticale boekenkast, zithoek met open haard met marmeren schouw, en een leeshoek. Opvallend is de bibliotheek met kolommen van meccano en exemplaren afkomstig van diverse antiquairs.

El proyecto ha incorporado diversas soluciones de diseño a este espacio que integra en una sola estancia el salón (marcado por el contraste entre los cojines de seda blancos y negros), el estudio con la estantería vertical, la zona de estar con chimenea y embocadura de mármol, y el rincón de lectura. Destaca la biblioteca, con columnas de mecano y piezas procedentes de diversos anticuarios.

les
grands
trans-
Parents

HOUSING RENOVATION IN **PASSEIG DE GRÀCIA**

Inés Rodríguez, Raúl Campderrich / Air Projects // www.air-projects.com

This home is laid out as a continuous space, dominated by a single feature: a tempered glass box housing the dining area, bar, cabinets, and shelves, which creates an effect of lightness and reflections throughout the apartment. An interesting element is the connection between the bathroom and the walk-in closet through an internal window.

Cet intérieur est disposé en un espace continu dominé par un seul élément : une boîte en verre trempé contenant la salle à manger, un bar, des rangements et des étagères, ce qui crée des effets de légèreté et de reflets dans tout l'appartement. Un élément intéressant est apporté par la connexion entre la salle d'eau et le *dressing*, au moyen d'une fenêtre intérieure.

L'abitazione è distribuita partendo da uno spazio continuo, dominato da un unico elemento: una scatola di vetro temprato che crea un effetto di leggerezza e riflessi in tutto l'appartamento integrando sala da pranzo, bar, armadi e scaffali. Degno di nota è il collegamento tra bagno e guardaroba tramite una finestra interna.

Die Wohnung besteht aus einem durchgehenden Raum, der von einem einzigen Element beherrscht wird: einem Kasten aus Temperglas, der den Eindruck von Leichtigkeit und Reflexen in der ganzen Wohnung hervorruft und in den der Essbereich, die Bar, Schränke und Regale eingefügt sind. Besonders interessant ist die Verbindung zwischen Bad und Ankleideraum durch ein Innenfenster.

De woning is opgebouwd uit een doorlopende ruimte die door slechts een element wordt beheersd: een ombouw van gehard glas die voor een lichte uitstraling met weerspiegelingen in de hele flat zorgt en een eethoek, bar, opberg- en boekenkasten bevat. De verbinding tussen de badkamer en de inloopkast via een binnenraam is bijzonder interessant.

La vivienda se distribuye a partir de un espacio continuo, dominado por un único elemento: una caja de cristal templado que crea un efecto de ligereza y de reflejos en todo el piso, y que incorpora el comedor, el bar, armarios y estanterías. Resulta especialmente interesante la conexión entre baño y vestidor a través de una ventana interior.

CELONA
360°

Floor plan / Grundriss / Plan
Plattegrond / Pianta / Planta

Section / Schnitt / Coupe
Doorsnede / Sezione / Sección

APARTMENT **PORTAL DE SANT ROC**

Marc Armengol, Laia Soler // marcarmengol@coac.net

This project arose from the remodeling of an industrial space, resulting in a highly compartmentalized living space with a strong presence of salvaged pieces on ceilings and walls, and in most of the furnishings. Sliding doors add flexibility to the layout.

Ce projet est né du remodelage d'un espace industriel, ce qui donne un espace à vivre extrêmement compartimenté, avec une forte présence de pièces récupérées sur les plafonds et sur les murs, comme pour la plupart des mobiliers. Des portes coulissantes ajoutent de la flexibilité à l'ensemble.

Questo progetto nasce dal recupero di uno spazio industriale che ha portato a un ambiente abitabile con grandi elementi divisori e una forte presenza di componenti preesistenti recuperati su soffitti e pareti, che ritroviamo poi anche negli arredi. L'agilità strutturale si ottiene grazie alle porte scorrevoli.

Dieses Projekt entstand aufgrund der Restaurierung eines Industriekomplexes, aus der sich ein unterteilter Wohnraum ergab, in dem an Decken und Wänden viele ursprüngliche Elemente sowie ein großer Teil des Mobiliars erhalten blieben. Die strukturelle Leichtigkeit ergibt sich dank der Schiebetüren.

Dit project is ontstaan naar aanleiding van het herstel van een fabriek met als resultaat een bewoonbare omgeving onderverdeeld in verschillende vertrekken en met oude elementen op wanden en plafonds die zijn gerestaureerd, net als een groot deel van het meubilair. De soepele structuur wordt verkregen dankzij de schuifdeuren.

Este proyecto transformó un espacio industrial en un entorno habitable fuertemente compartimentado en el que destacan elementos antiguos recuperados en techos y paredes, así como numerosos muebles restaurados. Las puertas correderas otorgan gran flexibilidad.

TRAPANI

Ballantine's

Artemide

APARTMENT IN **EL PUTXET**

Eduard Samsó

This apartment in a hillside district of Barcelona features a functional spatial layout, where a single floor was given a split level design in order to compartmentalize the spaces and separate the different areas. The result is a modern and hi-tech home.

Cet appartement des hauteurs de Barcelone présente une disposition fonctionnelle : l'étage unique a été fragmenté en plusieurs niveaux afin de compartimenter les espaces et de différencier les secteurs d'activité. Le résultat est un intérieur moderne et *high-tech*.

Questo appartamento nella zona alta di Barcellona si impone per l'utilizzo funzionale dello spazio, distribuito su un solo piano che è però strutturato su vari livelli come tecnica di suddivisione e isolamento delle varie zone. Si ottiene così un appartamento moderno ad alto contenuto tecnologico.

Dieses Apartment im höher gelegenen Teil von Barcelona fällt durch die funktionelle Raumnutzung auf. Die Wohnung erstreckt sich über ein einziges Stockwerk, wird aber zur Aufteilung und Abgrenzung der diversen Bereiche durch verschiedene Ebenen strukturiert. Das Ergebnis ist ein modernes Apartment mit gehobener Technologie.

Dit appartement in een hooggelegen wijk van Barcelona valt op vanwege de functionele benutting van de ruimte, die uit een verdieping bestaat maar is onderverdeeld in diverse niveaus als techniek om de verschillende zones te scheiden en af te zonderen. Het resultaat is een modern appartement met een hoog technologisch gehalte.

Este apartamento en la zona alta de Barcelona destaca por el aprovechamiento funcional del espacio, dispuesto en una sola planta pero estructurado en diversos niveles con el fin de configurar las diferentes zonas. El resultado es un apartamento moderno y equipado con la última tecnología.

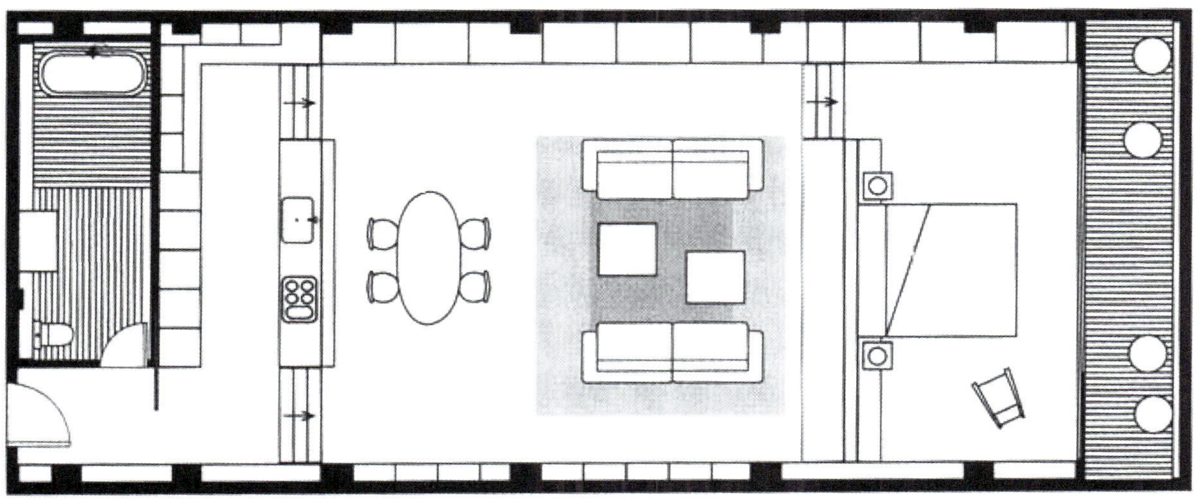

Floor plan / Grundriss / Plan
Plattegrond / Pianta / Planta

LOFT **PASSATGE DEL SUCRE**

Jordi Garcés, Berta Rovira // www.jordigarces.com
Interior and Furniture Design: Josep Cano / Loftbcn // www.loftbcn.com

After its restoration, an old distillery located in the Barcelona district of Poblenou was converted into a two-story home of singular interiors, where deep respect has been shown for the existing space. The Longwood pine trusses of the original structure were retained, adding special character to the upper floor.

Après sa restauration, une ancienne distillerie située dans le quartier de Poblenou, à Barcelone, a été transformée en un appartement sur deux niveaux où l'on a scrupuleusement respecté l'espace préexistant. On a gardé les fermes en bois de pin de la structure d'origine, ce qui ajoute un caractère particulier à l'étage supérieur.

Dopo un intervento di ristrutturazione, un'antica distilleria ubicata nel cuore del quartiere di Poblenou a Barcellona si è trasformata in questo appartamento a due piani dagli interni molto particolari, in cui emerge un profondo rispetto per lo spazio preesistente. È stato mantenuto un giunto in legno di pino della struttura originaria, che imprime un carattere speciale al primo piano.

Nach ihrer Renovierung verwandelte sich eine ehemalige Brennerei im Stadtteil Poblenou in Barcelona in diese einzigartige Maisonettewohnung, in der die alten Raumstrukturen sehr offensichtlich respektiert wurden. Die Erhaltung der Originalstruktur eines Gebälks aus Melis-Holz verleiht dem ersten Stockwerk seinen besonderen Charakter.

Na de restauratie werd een voormalige distilleerderij gelegen in het hart van de Barcelonese wijk Poblenou omgebouwd tot deze duplex met een bijzonder interieur, waar een diep respect voor de vooraf bestaande ruimte naar voren komt. Inlegwerk van moerasdennenhout is van de originele structuur bewaard gebleven. Dit verleent een bijzonder karakter aan de eerste verdieping.

La rehabilitación ha transformado una antigua destilería ubicada en el barrio barcelonés de Poblenou en un dúplex de interiores singulares, en los que se pone de manifiesto un profundo respeto por el espacio preexistente. Se ha mantenido una encaballada de madera de melis de la estructura original, que imprime un carácter especial a la primera planta.

Cocina sana

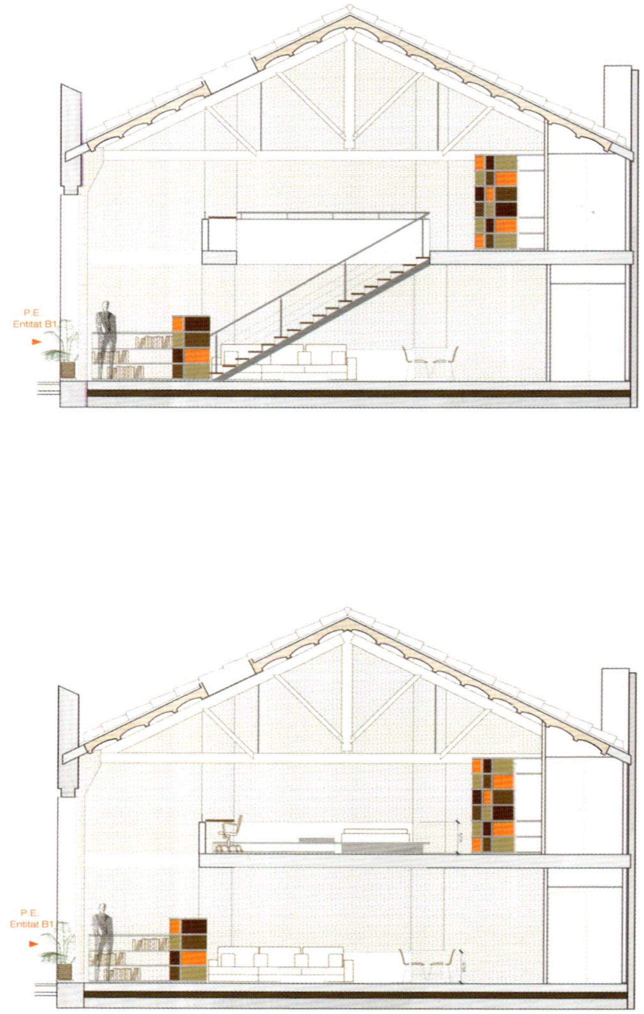

Sections / Schnitte / Coupes
Doorsneden / Sezioni / Secciones

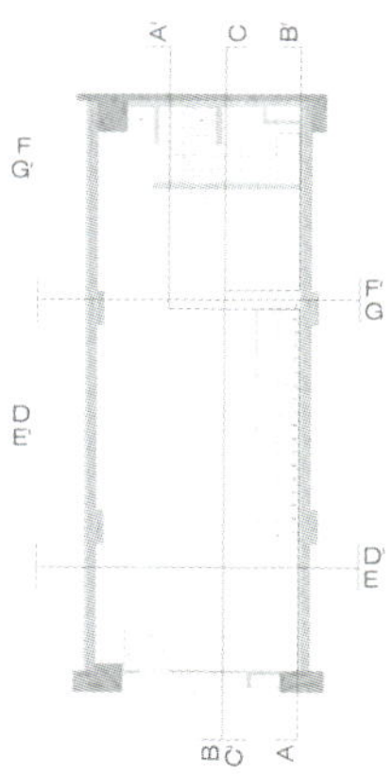

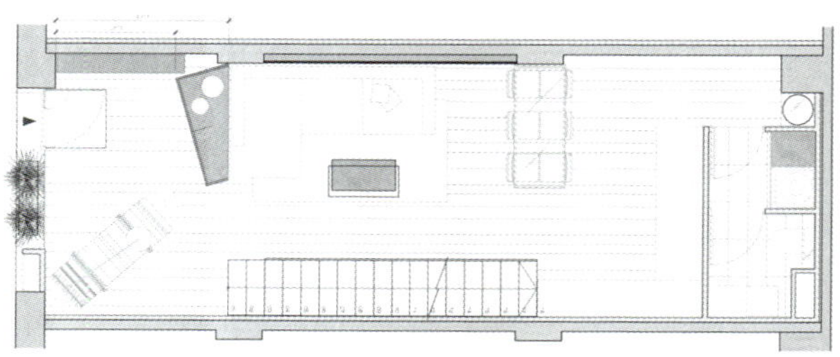

Ground floor / Erdgeschoss / Rez-de-chaussée
Begane grond / Piano terra/ Planta baja

Second floor / Zweites Obergeschoss / Second niveau
Tweede verdieping / Secondo piano / Segunda planta

Cocina
sana

Ray

LOFTS

APARTMENT IN **SANT FELIU**

Meritxell Ribé Modol, Josep Puigdomènech / Estudi Meritxell Ribé //
www.meritxellribe.com

The organization of the rooms is based on a traditional division: common spaces on the lower floor and private spaces on the top floor. The objectives of this interior design are, firstly to further enhance the light entering the interior thanks to its southerly aspect, and secondly, to integrate the terrace on all sides with the interior.

L'organisation des pièces respecte la division traditionnelle : espaces communs en bas, espaces privés en haut. Le but du concept est d'abord de mettre en valeur la lumière pénétrant à l'intérieur en raison de son exposition au sud, ensuite d'intégrer dans l'espace intérieur la terrasse pourtournante.

L'organizzazione delle stanze si basa su una distribuzione tradizionale: spazi comuni al piano inferiore e privati al superiore. Gli obiettivi di questa decorazione sono, da un lato, potenziare ancor di più la luce che penetra all'interno grazie alla sua orientazione Sud e, dall'altro, integrare la terrazza aperta con l'interno.

Hier basiert die Anordnung der Räume auf einem traditionellen Schema: die Gemeinschaftsräume befinden sich in der unteren Etage, private Räume im ersten Geschoss. Die Schwerpunkte bei der Gestaltung dieser Wohnumgebung wurden einerseits auf die Verstärkung des von Süden einfallenden Lichts und andererseits auf die Verbindung der nach allen Seiten offenen Terrasse mit dem Wohnungsinneren gelegt.

De ruimtes zijn op traditionele wijze ingedeeld: de gemeenschappelijke ruimtes liggen op de benedenverdieping en de privé-vertrekken op de bovenste. De inrichting had enerzijds tot doel de lichtinval, dankzij de ligging op het zuiden, nog meer te versterken, en anderzijds het omringende terras te integreren in het interieur.

La organización de las estancias se basa en una distribución tradicional: espacios comunes en la planta baja y privados en la superior. Los objetivos de este interiorismo son, por un lado, potenciar todavía más la luz que penetra en el interior gracias a su orientación al sur, y por otro, integrar la terraza a cuatro vientos en el interior.

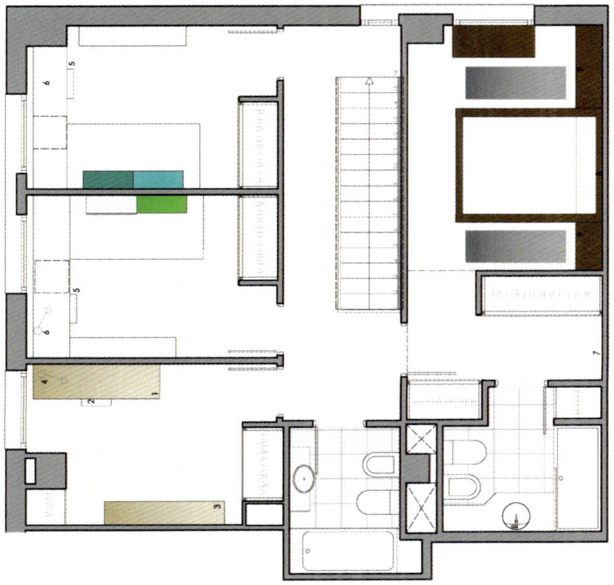

Ground floor / Erdgeschoss / Rez-de-chaussée
Begane grond / Piano terra/ Planta baja

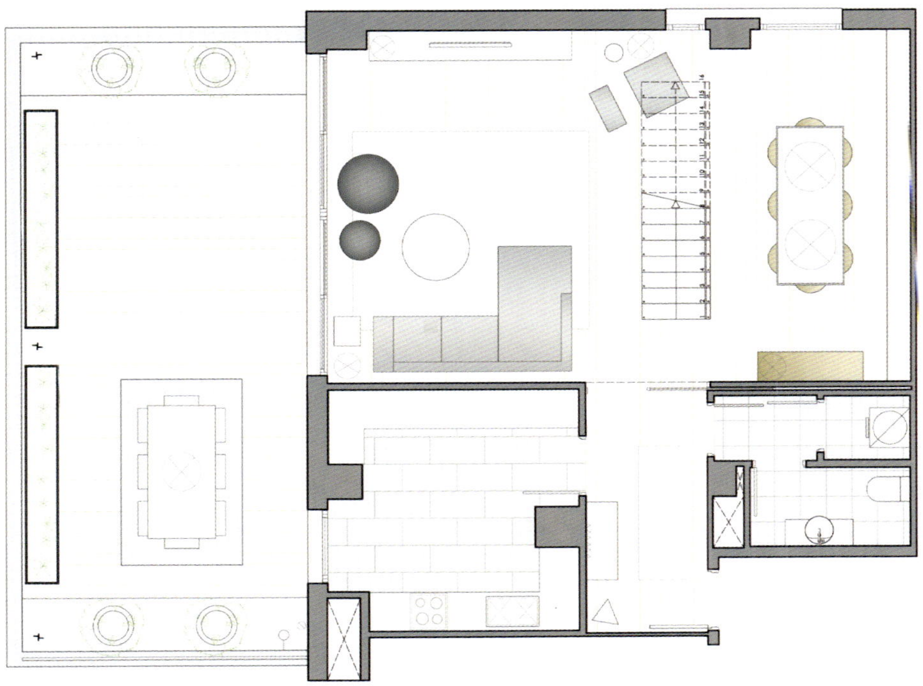

Second floor / Zweites Obergeschoss / Second niveau
Tweede verdieping / Secondo piano / Segunda planta

VOSS
VOSS

APARTMENT **CAN FELIPA**

Josep Cano / Loftbcn // www.loftbcn.com

In this loft, there are features from the industrial past along with other notable contemporary elements. Respect for what already exists has focused on the recovery of the brick and the lounge windows, whose height allows for a massive influx of natural light. An L-shaped attic surrounds the lounge and optimally distributes the space.

Dans ce loft, des éléments du passé industriel se mêlent à des éléments résolument contemporains. Le respect pour ce qui existait s'est concentré sur la récupération de la brique et des fenêtres du salon, dont la hauteur permet une entrée massive de lumière. Un attique en L entoure le salon et distribue l'espace à merveille.

In questo loft convivono elementi del passato industriale con altri di notevole contemporaneità. Il rispetto per il preesistente si riscontra nel recupero del mattone e delle finestre del salone, la cui altezza permette una entrata massiva di luce naturale. Una soffitta perimetrale a forma di L avvolge il salone e distribuisce ottimamente lo spazio.

Dieses Loft vereint Elemente aus der Industriegeschichte mit zeitgenössischen Details. Der Erhalt der bereits vorhandenen Strukturen zeigt sich in den freigelegten Ziegelmauern und den Wohnzimmerfenstern, die dank ihrer besonderen Höhe viel Tageslicht einfallen lassen. Im Wohnzimmer teilt ein L-förmiges Zwischengeschoss den Raum optimal ein.

In deze loft staan onderdelen uit het industriële verleden naast elementen met een duidelijk eigentijds karakter. Bestaande delen zijn gespaard gebleven, hetgeen het beste naar voren komt in de bakstenen en in de ramen van de zitkamer die dankzij hun hoogte veel daglicht naar binnen laten. Een L-vormige tussenverdieping langs de omtrek van de zitkamer zorgt voor een optimale indeling van de ruimte.

En este loft conviven elementos del pasado industrial con otros de notable contemporaneidad. El respeto por lo antiguo se ha centrado en la recuperación del ladrillo y las ventanas del salón, cuya altura permite que entre abundante luz natural. Un altillo perimetral en forma de L envuelve el salón y distribuye óptimamente el espacio.

Coronita

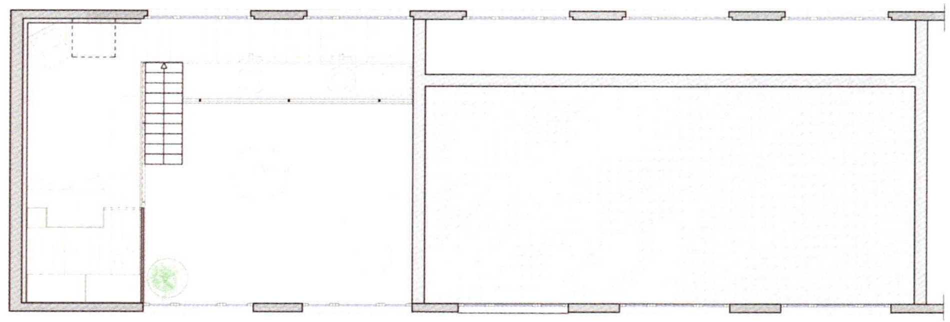

Mezzanine / Zwischengeschoss / Mezzanine
Tussenverdiepingen / Mezzanino / Entreplanta

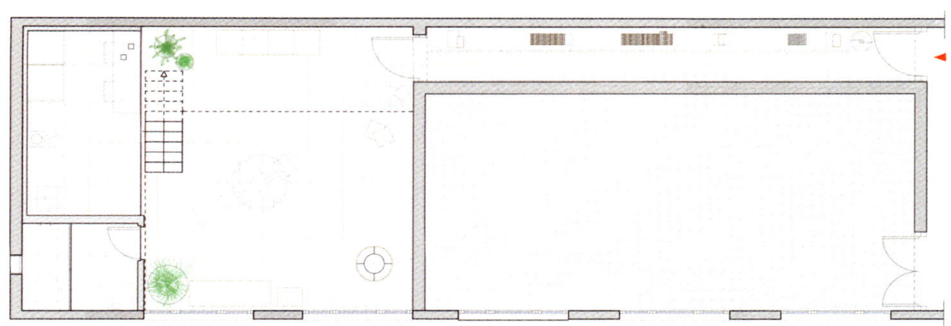

Ground floor / Erdgeschoss / Rez-de-chaussée
Begane grond / Piano terra/ Planta baja

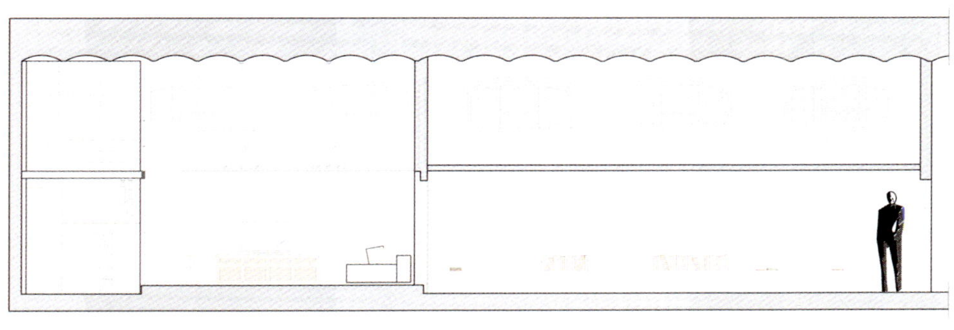

Longitudinal section / Längsschnitt / Coupe longitudinale
Lengtedoorsnede / Sezione longitudinale / Sección longitudinal

Use of space:
It is important that the furnishing and architectural elements of small spaces should be functional and as coherently and comfortably laid out as possible.

Raumnutzung:
In kleinen Räumen ist es wichtig, dass alle architektonischen Elemente und Einrichtungsgegenstände eine Funktion erfüllen und so stimmig und komfortabel wie möglich angeordnet werden.

Utilisation de l'espace :
Il est important que le mobilier et les éléments d'architecture des petits espaces intérieurs soient fonctionnels et agencés aussi confortablement et logiquement que possible.

Ruimtebenutting:
In kleine ruimten is het belangrijk dat alle elementen van het meubilair en de architectonische aspecten functioneel en zo coherent en comfortabel mogelijk verdeeld zijn.

Uso dello spazio:
Negli spazi piccoli è importante che tutti gli elementi di arredo e architettonici siano funzionali e distribuiti nel modo più coerente e comodo possibile.

Uso del espacio:
En los espacios pequeños es importante que todos los elementos del mobiliario y arquitectónicos sean funcionales y estén distribuidos de la forma más coherente y cómoda posible.

Integrated spaces:
Integrating living and dining areas with the kitchen is a highly attractive solution. This can be done fully, by means of a glass partition, or in a transitory manner with an intermediate breakfast bar or table.

Integrierte Räume:
Eine sehr attraktive Lösung besteht oftmals darin, die Küche in das Wohn- und Esszimmer zu integrieren. Man kann die Bereiche z. B. mithilfe einer Glaswand, eines Tresens oder eines Tisches voneinander abgrenzen.

Espaces intégrés :
L'intégration du séjour, de la salle à manger et de la cuisine constitue une solution extrêmement séduisante. Cela est parfaitement réalisable, au moyen d'une cloison de verre – ou de façon transitoire par le biais d'une table ou d'un comptoir de petit-déjeuner.

Geïntegreerde ruimtes:
De keuken opnemen in de woonkamer blijkt een zeer aantrekkelijke oplossing te zijn. Er kan gebruik gemaakt worden van een totale integratie met bijvoorbeeld een glazen tussenwand, of een tijdelijke door er een bar of tafel tussen te zetten.

Spazi integrati:
Integrare il salotto, la sala da pranzo e la zona giorno con la cucina è una soluzione molto interessante. Lo si può fare in modo totale utilizzando un divisorio di vetro oppure con una soluzione temporanea aggiungendo un bancone o un tavolo intermedio.

Espacios integrados:
Integrar el salón, el comedor y la zona de estar con la cocina resulta una solución muy atractiva. Se puede hacer de forma total, mediante un separador de cristal, o transitoria, mediante una barra o mesa intermedia.

Separation of spaces:
Many tricks can be used to separate spaces. One of the most common is to positioning a bookcase or unit as a partition between the living area and the entrance hall, or placing curtains/screens with little optical weight. These can provide a permanent or provisional separation, as required.

Abtrennen einzelner Bereiche:
Es gibt viele Möglichkeiten, wie man verschiedene Bereiche voneinander abtrennen kann. Zu dem an häufigsten eingesetzten Lösungen gehören das Aufstellen eines Bücherregals, um beispielsweise das Wohnzimmer vom Eingangsbereich abzugrenzen, und das Anbringen von Vorhängen bzw. Wandschirmen, dank derer ohne großes optisches Gewicht eine dauernde oder, falls gewünscht, zeitweilige Abteilung erzielt wird.

Séparation des espaces :
De nombreuses resscurces peuvent être mises en œuvre pour séparer les espaces. L'une des plus courantes est d'installer une bibliothèque ou une unité de rangement (étagères) entre l'entrée et le séjour, voire de disposer des écrans ou des rideaux sans lourdeur optique. La séparation ainsi obtenue peut alors être permanente ou transitoire, en fonction des besoins.

Afscheiding van ruimtes:
Er zijn vele mogelijkheden om ruimten van elkaar te scheiden. Een van de gebruikelijkste is het plaatsen van een (boeken-) kast om de woonkamer van de hal te scheiden, of door het gebruik van gordijnen/kamerschermen. Hiermee wordt een permanente of, desgewenst, een tijdelijke scheiding met nauwelijks optisch gewicht verkregen.

Separazione degli spazi:
Sono molte le soluzioni impiegate per separare gli spazi. Una delle più comuni è quella di posizionare un mobile-libreria per rendere autonoma la zona del salone e dell'ingresso oppure sistemare tende/paraventi con cui, senza alcun appensantimento visivo, è possibile ottenere una divisione permanente o, se lo si desidera, temporanea.

Separación de espacios:
Son muchos los recursos que se emplean para la separación de espacios. Uno de los más habituales es situar un mueble-librería para independizar salón y recibidor, o colocar cortinas/biombos, con los que, sin apenas peso óptico, se consigue una división permanente o, si se desea, temporal.

Glass partitions:
Glass partitions can enhance the feeling of space and light as they allow natural daylight to pass.

Gläserne Trennwände:
Zwischenwände aus Glas tragen dazu bei, den Eindruck von Großräumigkeit zu erwecken und die Umgebung zu erhellen, da sie Tageslicht einfallen lassen.

Cloisons de verre :
Des cloisons de verre peuvent améliorer ou mettre en valeur la sensation d'espace et de lumière, car elles permettent une meilleure pénétration de la lumière naturelle.

Glaspanelen:
Glazen tussenschotten helpen mee om het gevoel van ruimte te verhogen en om de verschillende delen te verlichten, aangezien zij de inval van zonlicht mogelijk maken.

Divisori in vetro:
I divisori in vetro contribuiscono ad aumentare la sensazione di ampiezza e a illuminare gli ambienti consentendo l'ingresso di luce naturale.

Separadores de cristal:
Los tabiques de vidrio contribuyen a aumentar la sensación de amplitud y a iluminar los ambientes, ya que permiten la entrada de luz natural.

Split levels:
Split levels provide separation of spaces, such as between living and dining areas, or between the master bedroom and other public spaces, without need for built partition walls, producing a feeling of space and light for the entire home.

Verschiedene Ebenen:
Unterschiedliche Ebenen erlauben es, verschiedene Bereiche voneinander zu trennen, wie zum Beispiel das Wohnzimmer vom Esszimmer oder das Hauptschlafzimmer von den gemeinschaftlich genutzten Räumen, ohne dass gemauerte Zwischenwände nötig sind. Auf diese Weise wirkt die gesamte Wohnung großzügiger und heller.

Niveaux fragmentés :
La fragmentation des niveaux procure une séparation des espaces intérieurs, par exemple entre le séjour et la salle à manger, ou entre la chambre et les espaces publics de l'habitat, sans avoir besoin de murs de séparation. Cette ressource produit une sensation d'espace et de lumière dont toute la maison bénéficie.

Split-levels:
Met hoogteverschillen kunnen ruimtes van elkaar gescheiden worden, zoals de living van de eethoek of de hoofdslaapkamer van de rest van de gemeenschappelijke ruimtes, zonder gemetselde tussenwanden. Hierrmee wordt ruimte en licht in de gehele woning verkregen.

Dislivelli:
I dislivelli consentono di separare gli ambienti come il salotto dalla sala da pranzo o la camera principale dal resto degli spazi collettivi senza necessità di pareti in muratura, ottenendo così un senso di ampiezza e luminosità in tutta l'abitazione.

Desniveles:
Los desniveles permiten separar estancias, como el salón del comedor o el dormitorio principal del resto de los espacios colectivos, sin necesidad de tabiques de obra. Así se consigue amplitud y luminosidad en toda la vivienda.

Sliding doors:
A good strategy for gaining space is replacing hinged doors with sliding doors.

Schiebetüren:
Eine gute Strategie, um Platz zu gewinnen, besteht darin, Scharniertüren durch Schiebetüren zu ersetzen.

Portes coulissantes :
Une bonne stratégie pour gagner de l'espace est de remplacer les portes à charnières par des portes coulissantes.

Schuifdeuren:
Een goede strategie om ruimte te winnen is de vervanging van scharnierdeuren voor schuifdeuren.

Porte scorrevoli:
Una buona strategia per guadagnare spazio consiste nel sostituire le classiche porte a cerniera con porte scorrevoli.

Puertas correderas:
Una buena estrategia para ganar espacio consiste en sustituir las puertas de bisagras por puertas correderas.

Multiple uses of a single space:
A single space can serve different functions. An example of this is a corner of the living area that is set up as a work space, or a dining room that turns into a bedroom.

Mehrfachnutzung eines einzigen Raumes:
Ein einziger Raum kann verschiedene Funktionen erfüllen, wie z. B. durch Einrichtung eines Arbeitsplatzes in einer Ecke des Wohnzimmers oder die Schaffung eines Esszimmers, das sich in ein Schlafzimmer verwandelt.

Espace unique, usages multiples :
Un seul et même espace peut servir à différentes fonctions. Exemples : le coin d'un séjour peut être aménagé en espace de travail ; une salle à manger peut être transformée en chambre à coucher, etc.

Veelzijdig gebruik van een enkele ruimte:
Een kamer kan diverse functies hebben. Zo kan bijvoorbeeld een hoek van de woonkamer worden ingericht als werkruimte of een eethoek in slaapkamer worden omgevormd.

Usi multipli di uno stesso spazio:
Una stessa area può svolgere varie funzioni come, ad esempio, un angolo del salotto utilizzato come zona di lavoro o una sala da pranzo che diventa zona notte.

Espacios multifuncionales:
Una misma área puede cumplir diversas funciones, como, por ejemplo, un rincón del salón que se habilita como zona de trabajo o un comedor que se transforma en alcoba.

Stairs:
The stairs in duplex apartments become a leading feature. The stairwell can also provide storage solutions.

Treppen:
Im Fall von zweigeschossigen Wohnungen werden die Treppen zu Schlüsselelementen. Außerdem kann man die vorhandenen Hohlräume auch als Stauraum nutzen.

Escalier :
L'escalier devient un élément-clé dans les appartements en duplex. Une cage d'escalier peut également fournir des solutions de rangement.

Trappen:
Bij een duplexwoning nemen de trappen een belangrijke rol in beslag. Daarnaast kan het trapgat worden gebruikt als opslagruimte.

Scale:
Nel caso di abitazioni distribuite su due piani, le scale diventano protagoniste. Il vano scale può inoltre essere sfruttato per soluzioni contenitive.

Escaleras:
En el caso de los dúplex, las escaleras se convierten en protagonistas. Además, el hueco puede aprovecharse para soluciones de almacenamiento.

Mezzanines:
Mezzanines are additional spaces created in apartments with high ceilings. A second level is typically built over the living area and is reached by means of a staircase that can also become a design feature. Depending on the ceiling height, this space can be used for sleeping, for storage, or as a study.

Zwischengeschosse:
Es handelt sich um einen zusätzlichen Raum, der in Wohnungen mit sehr hohen Decken geschaffen wird. Diese zweite Ebene wird normalerweise über dem Wohnzimmer errichtet und ist über eine mehr oder weniger auffallende Treppe zugänglich. Je nach Deckenhöhe kann dieser Raum zum Schlafen, für die Aufbewahrung oder als Arbeitszimmer genutzt werden.

Mezzanines :
Les mezzanines sont des espaces additionnels que l'on peut créer dans des appartements dotés de plafonds élevés. Le second niveau est fréquemment aménagé au-dessus du séjour et l'on y accède par un escalier qui peut aussi devenir un élément de décoration intérieure. Selon la hauteur de plafond dont on dispose, cet espace ajouté peut être utilisé pour le rangement, l'étude ou le couchage.

Tussenverdiepingen:
Het gaat om een extra ruimte die wordt gecreëerd in appartementen met hoge plafonds. Deze tussenverdieping wordt gewoonlijk boven de woonkamer gebouwd en is bereikbaar via een trap die al dan niet een prominente plaats inneemt. Afhankelijk van de hoogte van het plafond kan deze ruimte worden gebruikt als slaap- of opslagruimte of als studio.

Mezzanino:
Si tratta di uno spazio aggiuntivo creato negli appartamenti dai soffitti molti alti. Questo secondo livello viene normalmente realizzato sopra il salotto e vi si accede tramite una scala più o meno importante. In base all'altezza del soffitto, questo spazio può servire per dormire, come ripostiglio o come studio.

Entreplanta:
Se trata de un espacio adicional creado en apartamentos con techos muy altos. Este segundo nivel se construye normalmente sobre el salón y se accede a él mediante una escalera de mayor o menor presencia. Dependiendo de la altura del techo, este espacio se puede usar para dormir, para almacenar cosas o como estudio.

Attics:
Low sloping ceilings with windows set into the roof allowing daylight to enter and offering a view of the night stars are typical features of these spaces.

Dachgeschosse:
Typisch für diese Art von Räumen sind schräge und niedrige Decken mit Dachfenstern, die tagsüber viel Licht hereinlassen und nachts den Blick auf den Sternenhimmel freigeben.

Greniers :
Des plafonds en pente, avec des fenêtres ou des vasistas ménagés dans le toit pour faire pénétrer la lumière, sont les caractéristiques courantes de ce genre d'espaces – qui offrent par ailleurs de jolis points de vue sur les ciels nocturnes.

Vlieringen:
Schuine, lage daken, die van dakramen zijn voorzien zodat overdag het daglicht naar binnen schijnt en 's nachts de sterren te zien zijn, zijn de kenmerkende eigenschappen van dit soort ruimtes.

Attici:
I soffitti inclinati e bassi composti da finestre a tetto che consentano l'ingresso di luce durante il giorno e di ammirare le stelle di notte sono gli elementi che caratterizzano questo tipo di spazi.

Ático:
Los techos inclinados y bajos, y que incluyen las ventanas en el mismo tejado, de modo que permiten entrar la luz del día y ver las estrellas de noche, son los rasgos característicos de este tipo de espacios.

Entrance halls:
Entrance halls and passageways are included in the general space of the home, providing internal transit. It is important to leave free space that allows movement from one side of the home to the other.

Eingangsbereiche:
Dielen und Flure fügen sich in den allgemeinen Raum der Wohnung ein und erleichtern den Zugang zu den verschiedenen Zimmern. Es ist wichtig, ausreichend Platz frei zu lassen, damit man bequem von einer Seite der Wohnung zur anderen gelangen kann.

Entrées et couloirs :
Entrées et couloirs sont inclus dans l'espace général de l'habitat, comme espaces de communication. Il est primordial de laisser un espace libre qui permette de se déplacer d'un côté à l'autre de l'habitat.

Entree:
De hal en gangen worden in de algemene ruimte van de woning opgenomen, waardoor verplaatsing in huis gemakkelijk is. Het is belangrijk om ruimte vrij te houden zodat doorloop van de ene naar de andere kant van het huis mogelijk is.

Ingressi:
L'ingresso e i corridoi si integrano nello spazio generale dell'abitazione facilitando il passaggio interno di chi vi abita. È importante lasciare spazio libero che consente il transito da un lato all'altro della casa.

Vestíbulo:
El recibidor y los pasillos se incorporan al espacio general de la vivienda, facilitando los recorridos internos. Es importante dejar espacio libre que permita el paso a uno y otro lado de la casa.

Terrace enclosures:
Enclosing a roof terrace is a good solution for making the most of available outdoor space. Enclosures can be partial or complete, and enable views to be enjoyed without the need for leaving the interior space. The furnishings are arranged depending on positioning of the windows.

Wintergärten:
Das Verglasen der Terrasse ist eine optimale Lösung, um den verfügbaren Außenbereich voll zu nutzen. Diese Verglasung kann teilweise oder über die gesamte Front ausgeführt werden und ermöglicht das Genießen der Aussicht, ohne nach draußen gehen zu müssen. Die Anordnung des gesamten Mobiliars richtet sich nach den großen Fenstern.

Terrasses fermées :
Clôturer une terrasse est une bonne solution pour obtenir le maximum d'espace extérieur. La clôture peut être partielle ou complète ; elle permet de bénéficier des points de vue sans avoir besoin de quitter l'espace intérieur. Le mobilier devra naturellement être disposé en fonction de l'emplacement des fenêtres ou des portes-fenêtres.

Terrasafsluitingen:
De afsluiting van het terras is een optimale oplossing om maximaal te profiteren van de beschikbare buitenruimte. Het kan om een gedeeltelijke of volledige afsluiting gaan. Men kan van het uitzicht genieten zonder naar buiten te hoeven gaan. Feitelijk is al het meubilair gericht op de ramen.

Terrazze finestrate:
La chiusura della terrazza è una soluzione ottimale per sfruttare al massimo lo spazio esterno disponibile. Lo si può fare in modo parziale o totale; si tratta di una soluzione che consente di godere dell'ambiente esterno senza dover uscire fuori. Infatti tutti gli arredi sono orientati in funzione delle pareti finestrate.

Cerramientos de terraza:
El cerramiento de la terraza es una solución óptima para sacar el máximo partido del espacio exterior disponible. Se puede hacer de forma parcial o total, y permite disfrutar de las vistas sin necesidad de salir al exterior. De hecho, todo el mobiliario se orienta en función de los ventanales.

Custom furniture:
Custom furniture is a practical solution for integrating walls into a space. A built-in shelving unit on a wall or custom countertops, for instance, can be used to gain visual space while increasing storage options.

Einbaumöbel:
Maßgefertigte Möbel stellen eine praktische Lösung dar, die die Wände nutzt, um sie in den Raum zu integrieren, wie z. B. ein in die Wand eingebautes Regal oder maßgefertigte Arbeitsplatten, die optisch für mehr Platz sorgen und zusätzliche Aufbewahrungsmöglichkeiten bieten.

Mobilier sur mesure :
Du mobilier sur mesure est une solution pratique pour intégrer des murs dans un espace. Des étagères ou des plans de travail sur mesure ménagés dans un mur permettent de gagner de l'espace visuel, tout en augmentant les surfaces utilisables.

Op maat gemaakt meubilair:
Bijzondere meubels zijn een praktische oplossing voor het gebruik van wanden die in de ruimte worden opgenomen, zoals bijvoorbeeld een gemetselde wandkast of werkbladen op maat, om zo naast opslagmogelijkheden visuele ruimte te creëren.

Arredi personalizzati:
I mobili personalizzati costituiscono una pratica soluzione che consente di utilizzare le pareti per integrarle nello spazio, come ad esempio uno scaffale in muratura sulla parete o dei ripiani su misura che consentono di guadagnare spazio visivo offrendo nel contempo soluzioni di contenimento.

Mobiliario a medida:
Los muebles especiales constituyen una práctica solución que pretende utilizar las paredes para integrarlas en el espacio, como, por ejemplo, una estantería de obra en la pared o encimeras a medida, para ganar espacio visual, además de posibilidades de almacenamiento.

Multifunctional furniture and storage solutions:
Furniture of different styles, shapes, designs, colors, and functions become strategic tools for keeping the home organized. The most common are ottomans that can be used as side tables, sofa beds and beds with drawers, swivel chairs and chairs on wheels, extension dining tables, and stools that serve as magazine racks, to name but a few.

Vielzweckmöbel und Aufbewahrungslösungen:
Möbel verschiedener Stilarten, Formen, Designs, Farben und Funktionen verwandeln sich in strategische Werkzeuge, die dazu dienen, Ordnung zu halten. Die üblichsten Einrichtungselemente dieser Art sind Ottomanen, die man als Beistelltische nutzen kann, Schlafsofas, Betten mit Schubladen, Drehstühle oder Stühle mit Rollen, ausziehbare Esstische, Hocker, die als Zeitungsständer dienen usw.

Mobiliers multifonctions et solutions de rangement :
Des mobiliers de différents styles, formes, couleurs et fonctions, sont des outils stratégiques pour l'organisation d'un habitat. Les plus courants sont les ottomanes (que l'on peut utiliser comme tables d'appoint), les canapés-lits et les lots avec coffre, les sièges pivotants et les sièges roulants, les tables à rallonges et les tabourets servant aussi de porte-journaux – pour n'en mentionner que quelques-uns.

Multifunctioneel meubilair en oplossingen voor bergruimte:
Meubilair in verschillende stijlen, vormen, ontwerpen, kleuren en functies worden strategische hulpmiddelen om het huis opgeruimd te houden. De gebruikelijkste meubels zijn de ottomanes die kunnen worden gebruikt als bijzettafels, slaapbanken, bedden met laden, draaistoelen of stoelen met wieltjes, uittrekbare eettafels, bankjes als lectuurbakken...

Mobili multifunzione e soluzioni di contenimento:
Mobili di forme, linee, colori, funzioni e stili diversi si convertono in strumenti strategici che servono a mantenere ordinata l'abitazione. Gli elementi più comuni sono i puff che possono essere utilizzati come tavolini aggiuntivi, i divani letto, i letti dotati di cassettiere, le sedie girevoli o con rotelle, i tavoli allungabili per la sala da pranzo, le panche che fungono da porta-riviste...

Muebles multifuncionales y soluciones de almacenaje:
Los muebles de distintos estilos, formas, diseños, colores y funciones se convierten en herramientas estratégicas que sirven para mantener el hogar ordenado. Los más habituales son los otomanes (que se pueden utilizar como mesitas auxiliares), los sofás cama, las camas con cajones, las sillas giratorias o con ruedas, las mesas de comedor extensibles, las banquetas que son revisteros...

Folding furniture:
Folding furniture makes the most of space. If there is no dining room in the home, a table with folding chairs is the perfect solution. Folding bunks are ideal for children's rooms or guest rooms. A folding table is also a good idea for the kitchen: you keep it folded while cooking and open it when serving breakfast, for example.

Klappmöbel:
Klappmöbel erlauben es, den vorhandenen Platz maximal auszunutzen. Wenn kein Esszimmer vorhanden ist, ist ein Tisch mit stapelbaren Stühlen die perfekte Lösung. Zusammenklappbare Betten sind besonders für das Kinder- oder Gästezimmer geeignet. Ein Klapptisch in der Küche ist ebenfalls eine großartige Idee: während des Kochens bleibt er zusammengeklappt und z. B. beim Frühstück leistet seine zusätzliche Fläche hervorragende Dienste.

Mobilier pliant :
Le mobilier pliant représente un excellent gain d'espace. S'il n'y a pas de salle à manger dans l'appartement, table et chaises pliantes constituent la solution idéale. Des couchettes repliables sont parfaites pour les chambres d'enfant ou les chambres d'hôte. Une table pliante est aussi une très bonne idée pour une cuisine : on la garde pliée pendant la préparation du petit-déjeuner ou du repas, on la déploie pour manger, par exemple.

Opklapbaar meubilair:
Met vouwmeubels kan de ruimte maximaal worden benut. Als een woning niet over een eethoek beschikt, is een tafel met invoegbare stoelen een perfecte oplossing. Inklapbare stapelbedden zijn ideaal voor kinder- of logeerkamers. Een inklapbare bijzettafel in de keuken is ook een goed idee: als er gekookt wordt blijft de tafel ingeklapt en voor bijvoorbeeld het ontbijt wordt hij uitgeklapt.

Mobili pieghevoli:
I mobili pieghevoli consentono di sfruttare al massimo lo spazio. Se non si dispone di sala da pranzo, un tavolo con sedie pieghevoli è la soluzione perfetta. I letti pieghevoli sono adatti nelle camere dei bambini o degli ospiti. Un tavolo aggiuntivo pieghevole in cucina è una grande idea: resta chiuso mentre si cucina e si apre, ad esempio, per fare colazione.

Muebles plegables:
Los muebles plegables permiten aprovechar al máximo el espacio. Si no se dispone de comedor, una mesa con sillas insertables es la solución perfecta. Las literas plegables son idóneas en la habitación de los niños o de invitados. Una mesa auxiliar abatible en la cocina es también una gran idea: se mantiene plegada mientras se cocina y se abre para desayunar, por ejemplo.

Color:
Color is a very useful tool for creating a feeling of space. A small room painted in saturated or bright colors can appear to be much smaller than it really is. Light and neutral colors create the feeling that a room is much larger.

Farbe:
Farbe ist ein sehr nützliches Werkzeug, wenn man einen großräumigen Eindruck schaffen will. Ein kleines Zimmer, das in kräftigen und auffallenden Tönen gestrichen ist, wirkt viel kleiner als es in Wirklichkeit ist. Durch den Einsatz heller und neutraler Töne wird der Raum dagegen größer wahrgenommen.

Couleur :
La couleur est un outil très utilisé pour créer le sentiment d'espace. Une petite pièce peinte de couleurs saturées ou éclatantes paraîtra toujours beaucoup plus petite qu'elle ne l'est en réalité. Inversement, des couleurs neutres et claires créent la sensation d'une pièce beaucoup plus grande.

Kleur:
Kleur is een zeer nuttig hulpmiddel om een gevoel van ruimte te creëren. Een kleine kamer die in zeer felle en drukke kleuren is geschilderd lijkt veel kleiner dan hij in werkelijkheid is. Met lichte, neutrale kleuren lijkt een vertrek veel groter.

Colore:
Il colore è uno strumento molto utile per trasmettere una sensazione di ampiezza. Una stanza di dimensioni ridotte colorata in toni saturi e vivaci sembra molto più piccola di quanto non sia in realtà. I toni chiari e neutri trasmettono invece un senso di grande ampiezza.

Color:
El color es una herramienta muy útil si se pretende crear sensación de amplitud. Una habitación de dimensiones reducidas pintada con tonos muy saturados y llamativos parece mucho más pequeña de lo que es en realidad. Con tonos claros y neutros, la estancia se percibe mucho más amplia.

Mirrors:
Mirrors that are strategically positioned or placed opposite a window can optically increase the sense of space and spread daylight throughout a room.

Spiegel:
Spiegel, die an strategischen Orten oder gegenüber von Fenstern angebracht sind, vergrößern den Raum optisch und tragen dazu bei, das Licht im ganzen Zimmer zu verteilen.

Miroirs :
Des miroirs judicieusement disposés sont très importants pour un habitat. Accrochés en face d'une fenêtre, ils renforcent la sensation d'espace et contribuent à diffuser dans l'appartement la lumière du jour.

Spiegels:
Spiegels die op strategische plaatsen of tegenover ramen worden gehangen, maken de ruimte visueel groter en helpen het licht door het hele vertrek te verspreiden.

Specchi:
Gli specchi sistemati in punti strategici o davanti alle finestre consentono di ampliare visivamente lo spazio e contribuiscono a diffondere la luce in tutto l'ambiente.

Espejos:
Los espejos colocados en lugares estratégicos o enfrentados a ventanas permiten agrandar visualmente el espacio y contribuyen a difundir la luz por toda la estancia.

Proper lighting:
Proper lighting, preferably daylight, is very important for a home. Creating a visual curtain with ceiling lights or spotlights is another strategy for separating spaces, such as the kitchen area. Other sources of light should be fitted at strategic points.

Richtige Beleuchtung:
Die richtige Beleuchtung – vorzugsweise durch Tageslicht – spielt in einer Wohnung eine sehr wichtige Rolle. Die Schaffung eines optischen Vorhangs mithilfe von Deckenlampen oder Lichtstrahlern ist eine ausgezeichnete Strategie, um einzelne Bereiche wie beispielsweise die Küche, abzugrenzen. Die weiteren Lichtquellen werden an strategisch günstigen Punkten installiert.

Bon éclairage :
Un bon éclairage, de préférence naturel, est très important dans un habitat. Créer un rideau visuel avec des plafonniers ou des spots est une stratégie possible pour séparer des espaces comme le secteur de la cuisine. D'autres sources lumineuses peuvent être installées à des points névralgiques.

Geschikte verlichting:
Een juiste verlichting, bij voorkeur door zonlicht, is erg belangrijk in een woning. De creatie van een visueel gordijn d.m.v. plafondlampen of lichtbundels is een andere strategie om ruimtes, zoals bijvoorbeeld de keuken, af te bakenen. De rest van de lichtbronnen worden op strategische punten geïnstalleerd.

L'illuminazione giusta:
Un'illuminazione corretta, preferibilmente naturale, è molto importante in una casa. Creare una separazione visiva attraverso lampadari a soffitto o fasci di luce è un'altra strategia per delimitare gli spazi come, ad esempio, la zona della cucina. Le altre sorgenti di luce dovranno essere sistemate nei punti strategici.

Iluminación adecuada:
Una correcta iluminación, preferiblemente natural, es muy importante en una vivienda. Crear una cortina visual, bien con lámparas de techo o haces de luz, es otra estrategia para delimitar espacios, como, por ejemplo, la zona de cocina. Las demás fuentes de luz se instalarán en los puntos estratégicos.